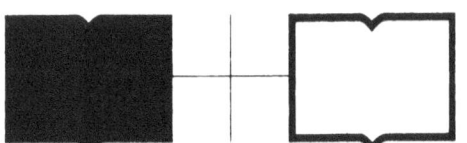 

Toronto Reprint Library of Canadian Prose and Poetry

Douglas Lochhead, General Editor

This series is intended to provide for libraries a varied selection of titles of Canadian prose and poetry which have been long out-of-print. Each work is a reprint of a reliable edition, is in a contemporary library binding, and is appropriate for public circulation. The Toronto Reprint Library makes available lesser known works of popular writers and, in some cases, the only works of little known poets and prose writers. All form part of Canada's literary history; all help to provide a better knowledge of our cultural and social past.

The Toronto Reprint Library is produced in short-run editions made possible by special techniques, some of which have been developed for the series by the University of Toronto Press.

This series should not be confused with Literature of Canada: Poetry and Prose in Reprint, also under the general editorship of Douglas Lochhead.

UNIVERSITY OF TORONTO PRESS

Toronto Reprint Library of Canadian Prose and Poetry
© University of Toronto Press 1973
Toronto and Buffalo
Printed in Canada
Reprinted in 2018

ISBN 0-8020-7525-8
ISBN 978-1-4875-8168-8 (paper)

No other edition located.

JEAN BAPTISTE
A STORY OF FRENCH CANADA

BY

J. E. LE ROSSIGNOL
AUTHOR OF "LITTLE STORIES OF QUEBEC"

LONDON & TORONTO
J. M. DENT & SONS LTD.
MCMXV

To
My Mother

LA RIVE NATALE

O patrie ! ô rive natale.
Pleine d'harmonieuses voix !
Chants étranges que la rafale
Nous apporte du fond des bois !

O souvenirs de la jeunesse,
Frais comme un rayon du printemps !
O fleuve, témoin de l'ivresse
De nos jeunes cœurs de vingt ans !

O vieilles forêts ondoyantes,
Teinte du sang de nos aïeux !
O lacs ! ô plaines odorantes
Dont le parfum s'élève aux cieux !

Bords, où les tombeaux de nos pères
Nous racontent, le temps ancien,
Vous seuls possédez ces voix chères
Qui font battre un cœur canadien !

Octave Crémazie.

CONTENTS

CHAP.		PAGE
I.	THE VOCATION OF JEAN BAPTISTE	1
II.	THE MIGRATION	16
III.	THE SORCERER	25
IV.	THE LOUP GAROU	35
V.	CASTLES IN SPAIN	45
VI.	THE HABITANT	54
VII.	HER MAJESTY'S MAIL	60
VIII.	THE CITY MAN	69
IX.	THE LOAN	80
X.	BLANCHETTE	95
XI.	LA FOLIE	104
XII.	PROFIT AND LOSS	115
XIII.	THE RETURN OF PAMPHILE	123
XIV.	THE TRIUMPH OF PAMPHILE	133
XV.	THE PASTIME OF LOVE	146
XVI.	THE TEMPTATION OF JEAN BAPTISTE	161
XVII.	VENGEANCE	173
XVIII.	MICHEL	186
XIX.	MOTHER SAINTE ANNE	200
XX.	THE ROBBERY	209
XXI.	LOVE AND WAR	218
XXII.	THE WILDERNESS	233
XXIII.	THE CURE	241
XXIV.	THE RELAPSE	249
XXV.	TREASURE TROVE	257

JEAN BAPTISTE

CHAPTER I

THE VOCATION OF JEAN BAPTISTE

"You may read, Jean," said Mademoiselle Angers; whereupon a breath of renewed interest passed through the schoolroom, as Jean Baptiste Giroux rose in his place and began to read, in a clear and resonant voice, the story of that other Jean Baptiste, his patron saint.

"Saint John, dwelling alone in the wilderness beyond the Dead Sea, prepared himself by self discipline and by constant communion with God, for the wonderful office to which he had been divinely called. The very appearance of the holy Baptist was of itself a lesson to his countrymen. His dress was that of the old prophets —a garment of camel's hair attached to his body by a leathern girdle. His food was such as the desert afforded — locusts and wild honey. Because of his exalted sanctity a great multitude came to him from every quarter. Brief and startling was his final exhortation to them: 'Repent ye, for the Kingdom of Heaven is at hand.'"

It was a simple and oft-repeated story, but there was something in the voice and manner of Jean that compelled attention. All the children listened; also the teacher; and the visitor, M. Paradis, curé of the parish, was visibly impressed. He brought his horn-rimmed spectacles down from the top of his head, set them firmly on the bridge of his nose, and regarded Jean for some moments without saying a word.

Jean returned the gaze with a steady, respectful glance; then let his eyes fall until they were looking at the floor just below the curé's feet. It was not polite to stare at visitors, but one might look at their boots. The boots of M. Paradis were covered with dust. He had walked all the way from the presbytery, two miles or more—that was evident.

" Ah, it is you, Jean," said the curé.

" Oui, Monsieur," said Jean.

" How old are you, Jean ? "

" Sixteen years, Monsieur."

" Sixteen years ! It seems like yesterday since you were baptized. How the time goes ! Sixteen years, you say ? You are no longer a child, Jean, no indeed. Well, it is high time to decide what we are going to make of you, certainly. Tell me, Jean; you admire the character of your patron saint, do you not ? "

" Mais oui, Monsieur."

" In what respect, my son ? "

" Oh, Monsieur, he was a hero, without fear and without reproach, like Bayard."

" Bayard, Jean, what do you know of him ? "

" He also was a hero, Monsieur. Mademoiselle Angers has told us about him."

" Without doubt. But Jean, Jean Baptiste, would you not like to be a hero like your patron saint ? "

" Oui, Monsieur."

" Forerunner of the true God ? Tell me that, Jean."

" Ah, Monsieur, as to that I do not know."

" You shall be, Jean, you shall be. Come, Jean,

come with me this instant. We will go to see your parents, that is to say, your mother. Your father, Jean, was a good man; he rests in God. Pardon us, Mademoiselle. I fear that we have transgressed. But it is a very important matter and I wish to speak to Madame Giroux without delay. Permit us, if you please, to go now. Will you not grant us this favour, Mademoiselle?"

"With pleasure, Monsieur le curé," said the teacher. "And I hope that you will find something suitable for Jean. He is a boy of great force of character, one who might be very good or very bad."

"True, Mademoiselle; it is always thus. Adieu, Mademoiselle. Adieu, my children."

"Jean," said the curé, as they walked along the winding valley road, "I have known you for a long time, since you were a very small child; and I think, yes, I quite think that you have the vocation, the divine call to the service of God and His Church. Yes, it seems to me that you have all the marks. See! *Probitas vitæ*, innocence of life. I have not heard of any real wickedness that you have done. Faults, perhaps, like all boys; transgressions even, but nothing serious; venial sins, merely, like all mortals.

"Again, *scientia conveniens*, scholarship. In that you are very strong for your age, assuredly. Mademoiselle Angers has told me that you are by far the most promising pupil in the school. Do not be proud, Jean; all that comes from God. Be glad and humble.

"Finally, *recta intentio*, sincere desire, pure and holy zeal for the glory of God, and the salvation of souls. Jean, Jean Baptiste, have you really these desires, these aspirations? Are you willing to give yourself to this holy work? Will you renounce the world, the flesh and the devil, and consecrate yourself to the service of God? Tell me, my son."

"My father," said Jean, hesitating and embarrassed, "I wish—I do not know what I wish. I would do something, I know not what. For the glory of God? Yes. For the good of man? Ah, yes. At least, for my relations, the neighbours, the parish. But to be a priest? No, Monsieur le curé, I cannot."

"But, Jean, you wish to attain the highest possible, do you not? I am sure that you do."

"Mais oui, Monsieur."

"Good, Jean, that is good. Then you shall be a priest. It is the only way to the excellence which you desire, unless you would follow the religious life. But you have no vocation in that direction, as I think."

"Monsieur!"

"Say no more, Jean. It is decided. Do not trouble. Here we are at your place, and we shall see Madame, your mother. Ah, there she is. Bonjour, Madame Giroux. We are making an early visit, are we not?"

"Mais non, Monsieur, you are always welcome. Be so good as to enter. Your blessing, Monsieur le curé, on us and our poor house. It is a great honour to have such a visit. Jean, place the armchair for Monsieur Paradis. Marie, bring a glass of cordial for Monsieur; also some of the cakes which you made yesterday. Monsieur Paradis, it is a cordial which I made myself last summer of wild cherries, and it is excellent for the stomach."

"Madame, the cordial is a veritable nectar, and the cakes are as the bread of angels."

THE VOCATION OF JEAN BAPTISTE

"It is Marie, Monsieur, who made the cakes. She is a treasure, that girl. I wish that all mothers could have such a daughter in their old age."

"You are indeed fortunate, Madame. And you have other daughters—Marguerite, Sophie, Thérèse, Agathe—I remember them well."

"What a memory you have, Monsieur le curé! Yes, five daughters, all married but this little Marie, and she will be going soon. Thus the young birds leave us, Monsieur, and begin to build nests of their own."

"But what a fine family, Madame! Five daughters and six sons."

"Pardon, Monsieur, seven in all. Little Jean, here, is the baby, the seventh."

"The seventh, Madame! That is lucky."

"Yes, Monsieur, the seventh son of a seventh. His father also was a seventh son, of a family of Chateau Richer."

"Madame, that is most extraordinary. It is truly propitious. The family Giroux, too, of Chateau—a well-known family in that parish, distinguished, even, of a most honourable history. But the younger sons, of course, must make their own way.

"Madame," continued Father Paradis, "this boy, Jean Baptiste, this seventh son of a seventh, was born, I am sure, to a notable career. Madame, I have visited the school, where I have heard him read in a marvellous way, while all the children listened with open mouth, and I said to myself, 'He should be a priest. I will go at once to obtain the consent of his good mother, for he shows all the marks of a true vocation to the ecclesiastical life. It is God who calls him.' Madame, you are happy in having such a son. I congratulate you, and I ask permission to send him to the college at Quebec and afterwards to the Seminary, that he may become a priest in the course of time, after ten years, perhaps."

For some moments Madame Giroux was unable to speak. Tears of joy coursed down her cheeks. Finally she said:

" This is a great honour, Monsieur le curé, for Jean, for me, for the whole family. How I wish that his father were alive to hear what you have said! I have prayed, Monsieur, to the Holy Mother, and I have asked this, but I have not dared to hope. Now I could sing, even in my old age, when my voice is gone. But do not fear, Monsieur Paradis, I will not. But truly, Monsieur, I could sing once, long ago. There was a time—but what am I saying? Ah, vain, foolish old woman, selfish too, to talk like that without regard to my poor Jean, who, perhaps, does not wish to become a priest. It demands a sacrifice to follow such a vocation. Jean, my son, do you really wish it? Are you content?"

" If you are content, my mother, I am content."

Thus it was arranged that Jean Baptiste should prepare for the priesthood and that he should go to college at Quebec in the month of September. It was a nine-days' wonder throughout the valley. On the following Sunday, after Mass, the neighbours stopped on the way home to congratulate the family Giroux, to ask questions, to criticise, to give advice. All the equipages in the parish were tied to the fence near the house, from the two-seated carriage of the rich farmer. Monsieur Taché, to the ancient haycart of Zotique Bédard, the last inhabitant on the valley road.

THE VOCATION OF JEAN BAPTISTE 7

Not since the funeral of Monsieur Giroux, five years before, had the family enjoyed such popularity. This time it was Madame Giroux who was the centre of interest; the mother, blessed among women, whose son had been chosen by the good God Himself to be His servant and priest. It was a great occasion. All of the cherry cordial was poured forth, and when that was gone, a barrel of spruce beer was opened, excellent and harmless beverage, which was drunk with joy to the health of Madame, of the young priest that was to be, and of all the members of the family Giroux.

Jean Baptiste had his turn on the following day at school, and for several days he was a personage among his associates. The teacher and the older pupils treated him with respect, while the younger children worshipped him like a god. Jean was exalted. He thought it a fine thing, like Joseph of old, to have the sun, moon and eleven stars bow down before him. Already he saw himself in the streets of Quebec, a full-fledged priest, in black hat and cassock, graciously returning the salutations of the leading citizens as he passed along. Now he was curé of his native parish, a man of power in the community, to whom all the inhabitants paid tithes, and before whom they all, from time to time, confessed their sins. Now he stood at the high altar, clad in gorgeous vestments, changing the bread and wine into the true body and blood of the Lord, elevating the Host, while all the people prostrated themselves before the good God and before his priest, Jean Baptiste Giroux. Truly, Jean had forgotten, or had never known, that pride goeth before destruction, and a haughty spirit before a fall.

The dominion of Jean over his fellow pupils was not

complete. Pamphile Lareau did not join in the worship of the new divinity, but scoffed at the whole performance. Pamphile was one of the emancipated. Had he not often visited his uncle, the cab driver, at Quebec, to whom priests, and even bishops were very ordinary persons? As for collegians, they were of no account at all. Had he not seen hundreds, yes, thousands of collegians, in their blue coats, green caps and sashes, promenading the streets like girls from a nunnery, two by two, a pair of ecclesiastics in front and a pair behind? Had he not thrown stones at the precious saints, and even mud; the nice sticky mud of the *Rue Champlain*? And what did they do, the holy ones? They wept, because their new clothes were stained with mud. Ah, bah! What was a collegian? And what was this Jean Baptiste, this sprig of divinity, this budding bishop, this little pope?

The children were fascinated by the conversation of Pamphile, though shocked at his levity in making mock of sacred things. He was jealous, evidently, since Jean could read so much better than he, and was in every way a better scholar, though nearly two years younger. It was a pity that Pamphile was so wicked, for he was certainly a fine young man, tall and handsome. But what would happen if Jean heard him talk? Jean was no coward, by any means, but of a fiery temper and very strong for his age.

While this discussion was going on Jean approached, and Pamphile began again, more violently than before.

"There he comes, the angel of whom we have been speaking. You will see, you others, what I will do to him."

"Ah, good morning, Monseigneur," said the young

THE VOCATION OF JEAN BAPTISTE

scoffer, with mock humility, bowing low before Jean. "Deign to inform us, if you please, why a priest wears a tonsure, why he has a bald spot on his head like an old man."

At the word "tonsure" the face of Jean Baptiste became suddenly pale. He had not yet thought of this aspect of his future career. The honour, the glory of it had appealed to him, but not the sacrifice, the renunciation. Unconsciously he passed his fingers through his luxuriant black hair.

"The tonsure, Pamphile, the tonsure? Truly, I cannot say. I do not know. I will ask Monsieur Paradis."

"You do not know, Monsieur the savant, Monseigneur the bishop, great fool, sacred sheep's head? Then I will tell you, simpleton. One wears the tonsure for the same reason that one has no beard, that one wears skirts, because one is no longer a man. Ah, Jean Baptiste Giroux, Girouette, you don't like that, eh? Ah, young priest! Ah, little saint! Ah, bah! I despise you. I spit upon you. There!"

Pamphile in his rage struck Jean in the face with his open hand.

In this Pamphile made a sad mistake, for Jean, usually of a peaceful disposition, was a lion when aroused. Forgetting his new dignity and all his holy aspirations, he flung himself upon his tormentor, seized him by the throat with both hands and shook him as a dog might shake a rat. Pamphile, in the fear of death, cried for mercy, and Jean, his anger giving way to contempt, threw him to the ground and walked away.

Presently, coming to himself, Jean ran back to Pamphile, helped him to rise, and said in a voice of great distress:

"Pamphile, I am a villain. I am sorry for this. You will forgive me, will you not, Pamphile, my friend?"

"Forgive you?" said Pamphile, with astonishing composure. "Oh yes, certainly. Say no more. It was all a mistake, my fault altogether. *Sacré bleu!* You are no longer a child. One must remember that."

It was thus that Jean Baptiste made his first enemy.

At the same time Jean discovered that he had another enemy—himself. For some days he had smothered his misgivings under his pious desires, his respect for the priest, his love for his mother, the pride of his own heart and the force of will that attaches itself to a decision; but now these misgivings arose with renewed power, and would not be put down. To be a priest, to wear the soutane, the tonsure, to be separated from the world, to hear confessions, to stand between God and man— all this seemed to him terrible and impossible. Better than his fellows he might be, but he would like to prove his superiority man to man, as in the struggle with Pamphile, and not by wearing a holy garment and an affectation of sanctity. And the vocation—what was it after all? Because he had a strong desire to do some good in the world, must he separate himself from his fellows? Was there no other way?

But when Jean thought of Father Paradis, all his doubts seemed to dissolve like the mist of the valley in the light and warmth of the rising sun. There was a good man, a noble character. What piety, what amiability, what wisdom! How useful to the parish, to the world, a priest like this! To be like Father Paradis—that were an ambition worthy of any man, sufficient, surely, for a mere boy like himself.

Thus was Jean Baptiste, like thistle-down, blown

about by every breeze, now rising, now falling, now suspended in mid-air, able neither to rise to the heavens nor to sink to rest on solid ground. It was a most unsatisfactory condition, and Jean found no peace for his soul. The decision that finally came to him is a curious example of the trifles that frequently determine the course of human life.

One afternoon, on his way home from school, where Mademoiselle Angers had been giving him advanced lessons in preparation for college, Jean was crossing the bridge of logs over the mountain torrent called La Branche, when he saw a little girl seated on the end of one of the logs, her feet dangling over the stream.

"Holloa, there, little red-head!" he called. "You will fall in the river if you don't take care. It is dangerous."

The "little red-head" made no reply, but gazed on the stream as though fascinated by the swirling water.

"Gabrielle, my little one," persisted Jean, "come away from that place. Are you not afraid of being drowned?"

"You know, Jean, you know very well that my hair is not red," said Gabrielle, looking up with a smile of mischief.

"May be not, Gabrielle. It is yellow, if you like, though it changes often. But come away at once. You frighten me."

"And I am not a 'little one' either, for I shall be ten years old to-morrow."

"True, Gabrielle, you are a young lady, almost. But do not fall in there, for the love of God."

"You are very strong and brave, Jean," said the little imp.

"It may be so, Gabrielle, but what of that?"

"You would save me if I fell in the river, would you not?"

"Gabrielle, you would not be so silly."

"Oh, I don't know. See me! One—two—three—away!" And Gabrielle was on the point of jumping into the stream, when Jean caught her, just in time.

"Little fool!" he said, pulling her up somewhat roughly and placing her in safety in the middle of the bridge. "Don't you know that it is dangerous, that place? See the deep pool and the big stones down there. It is not at all certain that I could have saved you. Never do that again. There now, don't cry. Run home to your mother, little one."

"You are rough, Jean, and cruel. Great beast! Leave me alone. I hate you." And Gabrielle turned away, weeping and sobbing.

"But, Gabrielle, what is the matter? What have I done? Poor little Gabrielle, do not cry. I am indeed a beast. Do not cry, Gabrielle."

But Gabrielle continued to cry, while Jean tried to console her in his stupid way. Finally she said, between her sobs:

"You are going away, Jean. You are going to college. You will be a priest."

"Well, and why not, little one?"

"I, I don't like that at all. Do not be a priest, Jean. Please."

"But, Gabrielle, it is a great vocation, that. See! I shall be curé of this parish, perhaps, and I will give you a lovely cross of gold, a pretty prayer-book and a rosary with beads of real pearls. And I will pardon all your sins, Gabrielle, if you have any, and not make you do any penance. Won't that be fine ? "

" No, no, Jean. I don't want any of those things. What good would they be to me if you were not here ? " Whereupon Gabrielle began to cry, more than ever, and would not stop until Jean promised, half in jest, half in earnest, that he would never be a priest, never in his life.

Then Gabrielle's tears disappeared, and she began to dance, and danced all the way home and into the house, chanting in joyful tones:

" Jean will not be a priest ! Jean will not be a priest ! He will stay with us ! He will stay with us ! Always ! Always ! "

" What is that you say, Gabrielle, mignonne ? " said Madame Taché.

" Jean told me so, truly. He doesn't want to be a priest, any more. And I, I am so happy."

" Be still, Gabrielle," said her mother, seriously. " That is too foolish. Jean will be a priest, of course, a bishop, too, perhaps, some day. Who can tell ? "

Meanwhile Jean went along the road toward his home with brisker step and lighter heart than he had known for some days. He saw the blue sky, the fleecy clouds, the dancing water of the river, the greens and purples of the mountains, the greens and reds and yellows of the fields. He heard the sound of the rapids, the song of the birds, the rustling of the leaves, the joyous chirping of many insects. He took long breaths of the pure mountain air, faintly scented with the fragrance of sweet-brier and wild strawberry. The very dust of the road seemed pleasant underfoot. The joy of living was his once more, and as he went he sang a song of life and youth, gay and free in the spring-time of the world.

> "Dans les prisons de Nantes,
> Dans les prisons de Nantes,
> Ya-t-un prisonnier, gai faluron, falurette,
> Ya-t-un prisonnier, gai, faluron, dondé.
>
> "Que personn' ne va voir,
> Que personn' ne va voir,
> Que la fill' du geôlier, gai, faluron, falurette,
> Que la fill' du geôlier, gai, faluron, dondé.
>
> "Elle lui porte à boire,
> Elle lui porte à boire,
> A boire et à manger, gai, faluron, falurette,
> A boire et à manger, gai, faluron, dondé."

"You sing, Jean," said his mother as she met him at the door. "You have good news to tell me, have you not? I like to hear you sing, Jean, my lad."

"Ah, my mother, I fear that it will not be good news to you, yet I know that you will understand. My mother, I cannot be a priest, never, never. I have wished to please you in this, but it is impossible. Do not be unhappy about it. You will not, will you, dear?"

"Jean, my son," said the good mother, "I am disappointed, of course, but that is nothing If you do not wish it I do not wish it. It is your happiness that I desire, Jean, my lad, nothing else."

The same evening Jean made his explanations to Father Paradis. The curé was sorry, for he had entertained ambitions for the lad, whom he regarded as a son, but he did not try to make him change his mind. On the contrary, he said :

"Jean, an ecclesiastical career without a vocation is

terrible. I have known several of those unhappy priests, and I would not have you among the number. It is well that you have discovered the mistake before it is too late."

As Jean walked homeward in the evening twilight his joyous voice awoke the echoes of the hills as he sang over and over that fine old song about the prisoner of Nantes and the gaoler's daughter who set him free. That gentle maiden, was her name by any chance Gabrielle ? Possibly, but it is not given in the song. Besides, the Gabrielle of whom he was thinking was only a little girl of ten years, and Jean himself was a mere boy as yet. But with the passing of the years what changes might one not see ? Be that as it might, one had to sing the song as it was written :

> " Que Dieu beniss' les filles,
> Qui Dieu beniss' les filles,
> Surtout cell' du geôlier, gai, faluron, falurette,
> Surtout cell' du geôlier, gai, faluron, dondé.
>
> " Si je retourne à Nantes,
> Si je retourne à Nantes,
> Oui, je l'épouserai ! gai, faluron, falurette,
> Oui, je l'épouserai ! gai, faluron, dondé."

CHAPTER II

THE MIGRATION

"What a big fool, that Jean Baptiste Giroux!" said Mère Tabeau, gossip and wise woman, as she sat on the doorstep of her cabin at the crossroads, smoking a black pipe and talking volubly to all the passers-by.

"What a fool he is to let slip a chance like that! Such chances do not come every day. *Mon Dieu*, what folly! To be a priest, that is well worth while; to live in a large, comfortable house, to receive tithes, to have everything that one could wish, plenty of good bread and butter, pea soup every day, potatoes, onions—all that. *Sapré*, I should like that, me. And what does he do? How does he earn his living? He prays all the time. An easy life, that. If only I could have what I want by saying prayers! *Nom de nom!* I say prayers, too, but what do I get? Some pieces of black bread, some morsels of fat pork, and this miserable hut."

"But that Jean Baptiste, what would he? He would like to be a great lord, to ride about on a high horse looking at his lands, his houses, his cattle, his people. Yes, it would be a pleasant life, a desirable existence. But those are dreams, imaginations, castles in Spain. In verity he will be a habitant like the rest of us, a cultivator who follows the plow, who feeds the pigs, who cleans out the stable. Ha! Ha! It is laughable. Those Giroux were always too proud, too far above us, too high, too mighty, and the good God did not like it. No, the good God does not love the proud, and He will bring them down—down to the dust. Already it has begun, the descent, but not yet finished. Wait, you will see."

At this point Mère Tabeau usually relapsed into silence, puffing away at her pipe until another neighbour came, when she would begin the same doleful song, with suitable variations. Thus public opinion was formed, by comment and discussion, until two conclusions were established: namely, that Jean Baptiste, though a great scholar, was a fool, with whom the good God would have nothing to do; and that the family Giroux were justly punished for having held their head too high.

Certainly Madame Giroux seemed determined to spoil her youngest son. All the other boys were obliged to work most of the time; but Jean, excepting in the busy season, had many hours for study, and was allowed to hunt and fish as much as he pleased. Father Paradis lent him scores of books from his library—books of theology, philosophy, history, science, belles-lettres— all of which he devoured with the greatest avidity. His appetite for books was insatiable, and often, during the long winter evenings, when the family sat about the big kitchen, the men smoking, the women knitting and chewing spruce gum, and all, as it seemed, talking at once, Jean would be seated at the end of the long deal table, reading by the light of a candle some leather-bound tome of which the very title was a mystery to the rest of the family. Naturally, Jean's brothers were sometimes piqued at the special privileges accorded to him.

"When is this going to end?" said brother Nicholas, one evening, to the assembled family. "What are we going to do with this book-worm? Is he going to be a priest? No. Then why does he want to read all the time? What is the use of that? For me, I call it foolishness. If he is to be a habitant let him work all day like the rest of us, and in the evening let him be sociable. Look at him, the lazy beggar, strong as an ox. Bah! What is the good of him?"

Jean made no reply, as became the youngest member of the family, but looked up from his book with a grim smile as though he would like to shake his brother Nicholas. But self-defence was unnecessary, for Madame Giroux took up the cudgels in his behalf.

"Let him alone, Nicholas," said the mother. "He does not wish to be a priest? Very well. That is his affair. But if he wants to have an education, he shall have it. Why not? It will cost nothing, and he will not need to spend ten years at Quebec. It may be well worth while—who knows? Perhaps he may become an advocate or a notary, but even if he remains a cultivator why should he not know something? I don't know much, myself, but I say that the habitants are too ignorant. Only the priests have knowledge. Jean, my lad, you shall read as much as you please, and if your brothers will not study they shall work. There!"

Yet Jean sometimes made notable contributions to the support of the family, for he was both hunter and fisherman, and when he brought in a bag of hares and grouse or a basket of trout his brothers had no complaint to make. He shot wild ducks and geese in the autumn, red deer and caribou in the winter; often he would trap a fox or a sable, and now and then he secured a wolf or a bear. The skins of these animals brought good prices at Quebec, and the meat was highly appreciated by the family and the neighbours as a pleasant change from the regular diet of fat pork. Certainly, Jean earned his living, and more, but got little credit because he did not do it in the usual way.

Thus six or seven years slipped away, while Jean led an existence free from care, like the grasshopper of the fable that sang all summer and thought not at all of the evil days that were to come. From the library of Father Paradis he got a knowledge of books such as few students obtain in all their years at college and seminary. From his work on the farm he acquired an extraordinary facility in the use of all the implements, especially the axe, the best friend of the backwoodsman. From his hunting and fishing expeditions he obtained a knowledge of woodcraft equal to that of an Indian, while he learned to know the beasts and the birds of the forest, the rocks, trees, wild flowers, and all the objects of Nature, as they are known to few naturalists. The growth of his body, too, kept pace with the development of his mind, until he was as fine a specimen of young manhood as one could wish to see, the like of whom could not be found in ten parishes. Truly, if education is the development of all the faculties, Jean Baptiste Giroux was a well-educated young man.

But, with all his talents, Jean was lacking in one thing, the desire to conform himself to the expectations of his friends, the will to fit himself to the scheme of things approved by them, sanctioned by long usage, hallowed by traditions handed down from father to son through many generations. He could have done it, but he would not. He had refused to become a priest, neglected to prepare himself for one of the other learned professions, and now there was but one career open to him—that of a habitant—unless, indeed, he left the parish altogether, as many of his friends had done. In the good old times a young man followed, as a matter of course, in the footsteps of his father. At the age of twenty he acquired a piece of forest land—there was always plenty of that—cleared a few acres, built a log cabin of one or two rooms, which he could enlarge when necessary, married a young girl of sixteen or eighteen, and devoted the rest of his life to the chopping of wood, the growing of hay, oats, and potatoes, and the raising of live-stock. At the age of sixty he was ancestor of a numerous progeny, a veritable tribe, destined to possess, in the course of time, a large part of Canada and a considerable footing in the United States. Thus the faithful did their duty by God and man, conquered the wilderness, possessed the land, and established themselves in the very gates of their enemies.

In some respects this was an ideal life, but the thought of it did not appeal to Jean Baptiste. He wished to do something different, he knew not what. In former times a youth of ambition and enterprise, such as he, would have turned *voyageur, coureur des bois.* Joining some band of Indians and trappers he would have plunged into the northern wilderness to make his way, in a birch canoe, by a chain of rivers and lakes, with portages short and long, to Lake St. John, Mistassini, Hudson's Bay, or even the Frozen Ocean. After many years, if he did not leave his bones in the wilderness, he might return, bronzed and battered, to his old home. With an Indian wife, perhaps, and money obtained from the sale of furs and fire-water, he would settle down among the scenes of his childhood and the friends of his youth to a life of ease, glorified by the memory of those years of travel and stirring adventure.

But times had changed. The Indian and the *voyageur* had passed away, and now adventurous youths, when seized with the spirit of the old-time rovers, would spend a winter or two in the shanties, work for a while in the coves and lumber-yards of Quebec and Ottawa, whence they drifted southward and westward to the factories of New England, the lumber camps of Michigan, the wheat fields of Minnesota, or the gold mines of California and British Columbia.

Thus the young men of St. Placide, the relations and friends of Jean Baptiste, kept going away one by one, always promising to return, but never coming back to stay. The home circle grew less and less, and the mother mourned her absent sons. Narcisse, the eldest and the first to go, was a carpenter in Montreal; Toussaint had taken up land in Manitoba; Bazile was working in the copper mines of Lake Superior; François was the owner of a cattle ranch in Alberta; and Hilaire, the last to go, was the farthest away, being employed in the salmon fisheries of British Columbia. It was a roving generation, descended from the old vikings and pirates of northern Europe, and the love of wandering was in the blood. During their early years they would stay at home, contentedly enough, but sooner or later they would hear the call and would go forth, with glowing eyes and courageous heart, to explore new worlds, to conquer other lands.

"Jean," said brother Nicholas, one day, " I should like to go to the North-West, to brother François, who has found a place for me. Soon I should have a ranch of my own and a hundred head of cattle—a veritable fortune, such as one could not get in a lifetime here. But I cannot go."

"Why not, Nicholas?" said Jean.

"Why not? *Mon Dieu*, Jean, you know very well. How could I leave the mother alone, that is to say with you, which is the same thing?"

"You can leave her with me, Nicholas."

"Leave her with you, Jean Baptiste? You, scholar, hunter, fisherman, good-for-nothing—what could you do? *Mille tonnerres!* You shall go to François and I will stay at home. But it is a pity, yes, a thousand pities. What a chance! *Sacré!* But you shall go, yes, to-morrow. I will not have you here. Do you understand, idler?"

"I will not go, Nicholas."

"What is that you say? You will not go? Refuse a chance like that? You refuse everything, everything. What obstinacy! The boy is a fool, an utter fool, beyond all hope. *Nom de cauchon!*"

"Nicholas," said Jean, earnestly, "listen to me. This talk about going away—I have heard it before, many times, every since I can remember anything. Fall River, Chicago, Manitoba, California—I am tired of hearing of them. Cotton mills, wheat fields, gold mines, cattle ranches—don't talk to me of all that. It is all very well to see the world, but why not try to do something at home? Why should all the young men go away, the best blood of the parish? Adventure, you say; enterprise? Why not have some of that here? See, Nicholas, the good land, the noble forest, the grand mountains, the lovely river! Where in all the world will you find a place more beautiful, more satisfying, where you would be more content to live and die? Are there no chances here, no possibilities? Perhaps not, but I will see, I will try. You others, all of you, may go, but I will stay. Yes, it is decided. Say no more, Nicholas, my brother. Fear nothing. François will be glad to see you, and the mother will be safe with me."

Nicholas was speechless. He had never heard talk like that, either from Jean Baptiste or any one else. The idea that distant fields were no more green than those at home was new to him and he could not receive it. Yet his brother's words inspired confidence, and he felt that he was going to have his way, as usual. As he well knew, Jean was strong and capable and always carried through what he began. Nicholas weakened, and referred the whole question to his mother, knowing well what she would say.

"Nicholas," said the mother, "you have a fine chance in the North-West, and I think that you ought to go. God knows that I would like to keep you all. But it is the way of life. The young birds leave the nest, and the mother with the broken heart—after a while she dies. But do not trouble about me. I am not going to die, no, not for many years. The good God and the Holy Virgin will watch over me. Go, Nicholas, with your mother's blessing. You have been a good son to me. There, I am not crying, not at all. I have still my baby, my little Jean. We shall not be lonely, shall we, Jean? But I shall never forget you, Nicholas, never. All the children have a place in my heart, and you, perhaps, more than the others."

"But, Jean," said the mother, when they were alone, "why do you wish to stay here? What can you do in this place, with all your talents, your education? I do not understand at all. Is it for my sake, or is there another whom you love? Jean, my lad, is it possible? Not Zéphyrine Boucher, she is too old for you; nor Mélanie Couture, she is not pretty at all; nor Blanchette Laroche—impossible. No, there is no one suitable in the parish, not one; not even the little Gabrielle Taché, who is much too young. But wait! The little Gabrielle grows older every year. One, two, three, four, five, six, seven—*mon Dieu*, how the time goes! She must be seventeen years old at the very least. And she is beautiful, of a good family, with a suitable dowry—no objection, none whatever. And did she not arrive from Quebec this very morning? Ah, Jean, you blush. I have found you out. It is for the sake of Gabrielle that you stay in St. Placide."

"My dear mother," said Jean, "you are laughing at me. Stay here for the sake of Gabrielle, that little imp with the red hair and freckles? Absurd! Besides, I have not seen her for years. She has been at the convent, I am told, learning music, painting, embroidery —all the accomplishments. She will be a great lady in the gay world of Quebec, quite out of my sphere, I assure you. No, my mother, there is no one whom I love half so much as you. Why do I stay in St. Placide? Truly, I do not know. For your sake? Certainly, most of all. Is there any other reason? Possibly. Who knows? All the others go away, and I, I will not. It is obstinacy, nothing else. There, my mother, I have confessed. Give me absolution now, and a kiss."

CHAPTER III

THE SORCERER

AFTER the departure of brother Nicholas things went on much as before. It was hardly to be expected that Jean would suddenly change his ways and settle down to the routine of habitant life after so many years of idleness. Miracles may be possible, but they seldom happen. Even Mère Tabeau acknowledged this, and the neighbours fully agreed with her. This proud young man would come to it in the course of time, but his spirit must first be broken. And that would happen —poverty would do it. He who was now promenading the countryside with rod and gun like a gentleman and a great lord would soon be grubbing in the earth. By and by his back would be bent and his legs crooked like those of any common man.

But Jean shocked the old gossip and the whole parish by employing a hired man. What sinful extravagance and folly! It was not as in former times, when one could get an able-bodied man for a shilling a day. Now one had to pay at least twice as much, while the rascals did barely half as much work, and demanded the best of everything—white bread, butter, soup, pork, and even eggs. And they would not sleep in the stable, as formerly, but wished to have a room in the house, a straw mattress, blankets, sheets, a candle to light them to bed—all the luxuries of modern life. But those Giroux people—how could they afford all that? Surely they were on the road to ruin, on the very brink of it. Presently they would be in poverty, and the parish would have to support them. Yes, it was a matter of public concern and somebody ought to interfere.

Nevertheless, Jean Baptiste kept the hired man, and, while working on the farm somewhat more than formerly, still found time for hunting and fishing and the reading of books, while his mother, as though bewitched, smiled complacently at everything that he did.

But Jean sank lower still in the estimation of the neighbours, for he began to keep bad company, the very worst—that of a sorcerer. It came about in this way. Jean was having a day's fishing, and, although the trout were rising well, he was not content to stay in one place but kept moving on up the stream until he found himself, at sunset, standing on a rocky ledge beside a deep, dark pool, called the *trou du sorcier*. Precipitous cliffs, crowned with firs and pines, rose on all sides, enclosing a sort of amphitheatre into which the river plunged in a white cascade. Striking a granite ledge, the stream swirled around in a great eddy, a dark whirlpool, on the borders of which lurked giant trout, old warriors that had broken the tackle of many a luckless angler, wary fish that must be under the special protection of Satan himself—so often had they escaped the toils. It was a place of evil repute, little frequented by anglers. So much the better, as Jean knew, for the man of courage, and, although he had never taken a large fish in the place, he was determined to try his luck once more in the famous pool.

Looking into the deep water at his feet he saw a sight that made his heart leap to his throat. It was the head of an enormous fish, the biggest he had ever seen, now pushed out from beneath the rock until he could see the gills, and the lateral fins, now slowly withdrawn until only the snout was visible. On tiptoe Jean drew back; with grim haste attached a new fly; tested the casting-line and the supple rod; and then, with a dexterous turn of the wrist, launched the fly upon the foam-flecked surface of the pool, just beyond the hiding-place of the trout. It floated down stream in full view of the fish, but the ancient denizen of the pool made no response, nor did any of the lesser fry dare to rise, but kept at a respectful distance from the king of the river. Jean made several casts, tried another fly, and another, until he had gone through his book; then put on a grasshopper; and, finally, descended to worms, but without avail.

"*Sacré!*" said Jean to himself. "This is a devil of a trout. What sort of bait does he want?"

"I will show you, Jean Baptiste Giroux," said a voice.

With an involuntary start Jean turned to see who had spoken, and was surprised to find himself face to face with the redoubtable Michel Gamache, *dit le Sorcier*. Michel was a man of sixty or seventy years of age, but tall and very straight, with the frame of an athlete, and the face of an ascetic, in which ferocity and gentleness were strangely blended. The high arch of the nose and the straight line of the overhanging brow made one think of a bird of prey; the shaggy, grizzled hair and the vice-like jaw gave him the appearance of an ancient wolf; but there was an expression of friendliness about mouth and eyes that attracted more than the harsh features repelled. He was bare-headed, and wore a brown blouse with trousers of the same colour thrust into the legs of long leathern moccasins, and he carried the usual fisherman's rod and pannier.

"I will show you, Jean," he said again, with the shadow of a frown; "that is to say, after you have done staring at me. You find nothing extraordinary in my appearance, I hope."

"No, indeed, Monsieur Gamache. I was a bit startled, that was all. But there is a trout down there, the biggest I have ever seen, and I cannot get him to rise. I have tried everything—flies, grasshoppers, worms—but he will not look at them. Now it is your turn, Monsieur."

"No, Jean; it is your fish. See, here is something that will fetch him. Try this."

Out of his pocket Michel drew a black, worm-like beast about an inch and a half in length, with jointed body and innumerable legs, and handed it to Jean.

Jean's eyes sparkled as he attached the wriggler to a hook, for he knew it well—the larva of the dragon-fly, deadly bait for all fishes in streams where they are found.

"That is very kind of you, Monsieur Gamache. Now we shall see. Here goes!"

Scarcely had the bait touched the surface of the pool when there was a rush and a splash and the big fish started back toward his hiding-place to enjoy the toothsome morsel he had so cleverly captured. Feeling the sting of the hook and an unaccustomed pressure on the jaw, he darted out into the middle of the pool, where he leaped from the water, turned a somersault in the air and lashed about like a harpooned whale. Then he plunged to the bottom and zigzagged up stream toward a mass of jagged rocks through which the water poured like a mill-race. Finding his progress slow he made another leap in the air, and started down stream, drawing out yards of line, and then came back with a rush, so that Jean was hardly able to take in the slack. It was a great struggle, with the odds in favour of the fish, for the angler's sole weapon was a light rod and a slender line, and the strain of the strong fish charging to and fro in the rough water was terrific. But Jean held the tip of his rod well up and exerted a steady pull to which the fish had to yield in the end. Slowly, but surely, Jean reeled him in, still tugging and circling about, but gradually weakening, until he turned feebly on his side, and his last struggles served only to land him on the rock at the angler's feet.

But the game was not yet played to a finish, for just as the fish was well landed he gave a last flop of the tail and broke the gut above the shank of the hook. Jean looked on as though paralysed, while his prize was slipping down the shelving rock into the water. At this point Michel Gamache ceased to be a neutral spectator, for just as the trout was slipping away, the old man, with extraordinary agility, pounced upon it, as a cat upon a mouse, seized it with both hands, and held it up, flopping and dripping, before the eyes of Jean Baptiste, who, a moment before, had been plunged in the depths of despair.

"Ah, Monsieur Gamache!" said Jean, with emotion, "you are a friend, indeed. But look at that trout. I have never seen the like—thirty inches at the least, and eight pounds. Yes, eight pounds, or more. *Mon Dieu!* What a fish! Magnificent! I never thought that such trout existed outside of *Lac des Neiges*. But look at that tail, those fins, and those spots—red, blue, yellow. Ah, my good fellow! Ah, cannibal! You will eat no more of your poor relations, nor frogs, nor mice, nor grasshoppers. You would not touch the grasshopper, but we found a good bait for you. Yes, Monsieur Gamache, it was you who did it. Certainly, you must be a sorcerer, as they say."

"Sorcerer, Jean Baptiste! You say that to me; you, the son of my old friend, Toussaint Giroux! He at least knew better than that; he, my friend, your father. But the times have changed, and the young people of to-day——"

"Monsieur Gamache, believe me, I did not mean it like that. It is only that I am grateful to you for the bait and for saving me the trout. It was truly miraculous. Yes, that is the word—miraculous."

"Well, Jean, that is better. You have some of the politeness of your father, as I see. Ah, he was a valiant man and a good friend."

"My father?" said Jean, in surprise. "I do not understand. He never spoke of it."

"Certainly not. That is what I say. He was a good friend and could keep a secret."

"A secret, Monsieur Gamache? That is interesting. But it is gettnig late and I must be going home. It was a good day's fishing. My pannier is full and I have that big one as well. But will you not keep him, Monsieur? He certainly belongs to you."

"But no, Jean; it is your fish, and I am glad that I had the honour of helping to catch him. But do not hurry, my young friend. Sit down a minute. I will tell you something."

Somewhat reluctantly, but without any fear of the old man, who was evidently disposed to be friendly, Jean sat beside him on the rock and listened to the story of former days before the family Giroux came to the parish of St. Placide.

"Your father, Jean, as you know, was a native of the parish of Chateau Richer, on the other side of those mountains. And I, as you do not know, lived in the parish of Ste. Famille on the other side of the Channel, in the Isle of Orleans—the Isle of Sorcerers, as they call it. It was not an isle of sorcerers at all, but I will tell you what it was—an isle of smugglers. Yes, smugglers. When the good people of Chateau, there below, saw those lights on a dark night moving to and fro on the long marsh, gleaming fitfully, like fireflies, they crossed themselves, the simpletons, and muttered, 'will-o'-the-wisps,' 'devil's fire,' 'sorcerers!' Ha! Ha! What foolishness! They were smugglers with lanterns going to meet a bateau at high tide, carrying casks of brandy and French wines, packages of tobacco, bales of silk, and all that. Nobody came near them, you may be sure. Very convenient, the Isle of Sorcerers, for smugglers, and there were fine hiding-places in the long marsh and on the side of the hill. Caves? Oh, yes, here and there. I wonder if I could find them now. Ah, those were days!"

"But you were no smuggler, Monsieur Gamache, nor my father either. Impossible."

"Nothing is impossible, Jean. All good is possible and all bad. We were smugglers, certainly, for fun at first, and afterwards for profit. Talk of farming, cultivating the soil—that is a slow way of earning one's living, not to speak of making a fortune. But free trade, smuggling, if you like, going out of a dark night in a little boat, slipping up the river with the tide, landing something on the quays of the St. Charles, slipping down with the ebb, arriving in the early morning to see the coming of the dawn, the lifting of the mist and the first glow of sunrise on the top of Mount Ste. Anne—Jean, it was glorious. I like to think of it. If only those days could come again!"

" And dangerous, Monsieur Gamache ?"

" Dangerous ? Certainly. That was the glory of it. But when one is found out one goes to prison, perhaps, or one crosses the mountains to the parish of St. Placide, where the past may be forgotten."

" Monsieur Gamache," said Jean, " I can well believe that my father was a smuggler, for people had different ideas about such things in those days, and the adventure of that life must have appealed to him, but as to the profit—that is not quite so credible. He was a poor man when he came to St. Placide, and the farm he created himself, cut all the trees with his own axe, dug the ground with a spade, carried hay and oats on his back up the hills. No, Monsieur, my father did not profit by the trade of which you speak."

" That is true, Jean, he did it for fun, for adventure, for the beauty and glory of it, and he would not touch one sou of the profit. But he took the punishment, the exile, just the same. Have I not said that he was a valiant man ?"

These were strange tales that Jean was hearing that night, beside that weird pool, while the stars came out, and the new moon rose above the circle of the trees and cast a trembling brightness on the water below. The sound of the river filled the air as though trying to drown the voice of Michel Gamache as he told of the lawless exploits of former days, when Toussaint Giroux and he were young and sowing to the wind. It was almost sacrilege in Jean to be hearing of such doings, yet he could not but feel a thrill of pride as he thought of his father, in the hey-day of life, high-spirited, strong and brave, going into danger with a smile on his lips and a brightness in his eye, glorying in adventure for itself alone, and scorning both the reward and the penalty. In his heart Jean was wishing that he had been there and hoping that like opportunities might come again. Evidently Michel Gamache was corrupting the morals of the son as he had formerly corrupted those of the father. Perhaps he was a sorcerer after all, a servant of Satan, the enemy of souls.

"You are late, Jean," said Madame Giroux, as the fisherman finally arrived at home. "You are very late, and I thought that you would never come. The river is dangerous in places. You remember Hypolite Picard, who was drowned last year. He could swim, too, but it is always the swimmers who take the risks. I wish that you would be more careful. Well, I am glad that you are safe at home. Sit down, now, and take some of this hot soup. I will cook a trout for you, if you like. You got some, of course."

"But certainly, my mother," said Jean, opening his pannier, "look at these."

"Truly you have a lot, about ten dozen, I should say. At Beauport we could get twenty cents a dozen for them, and at the Champlain market in Quebec at least five cents more. Two dollars' worth of fish—not a bad day's work. But what have you there, behind your back? *Mon Dieu!* What is that? A salmon, a whale! What a monster! You are a fisherman indeed! How I wish that your father were here to see that trout! He caught one once about the same size, but I have never since seen its equal. That was when we first came to St. Placide, forty years ago. We were young then. But where did you get it? In some deep hole, no doubt."

"Yes, my mother, in the *Trou du Sorcier*."

"God guard us!" said Madame Giroux, crossing herself. "The *Trou du Sorcier*, the very place where your father caught that other fish. And the sorcerer himself, was he there, perhaps, as then?"

"Yes, my mother, he was there. That is curious, is it not? But he is no sorcerer, only an old man, most obliging and interesting."

"The devil is always interesting, Jean, and obliging too, for a time. But if this man is not a sorcerer he is a thief, certainly, and a miser. Besides, he never goes to Mass—has not made his Easter confession in forty years. If he should die suddenly Satan would surely take his soul. Jean, I am not superstitious, not at all, but I think that we should send the fish to the curé."

Thus it happened that Father Paradis had a good dinner on the next day, which was Friday, and for several days thereafter the good curé and his housekeeper made their breakfast, dinner and supper of baked trout.

CHAPTER IV

THE LOUP GAROU

"*Bon soir*, Jean Baptiste," said Mère Tabeau one evening, as the young man passed her home on his way to visit his friend Michel Gamache.

"*Bon soir, Madame*," said Jean, politely, but not stopping, as he sometimes did, to gossip with the old woman

"Not so fast, Jean. Wait a minute. I have something to tell you. Come here."

"Another time, Madame Tabeau, if you please. I must hasten this evening."

"No time!" cackled the old crone in a shrill, querulous voice. "No time to talk to a poor old woman; no time for that, oh, no! But time enough for your friend the sorcerer, that servant of the devil."

"Madame Tabeau, take care what you say. You speak of Monsieur Gamache, no doubt. He is old, perhaps, and not at all handsome, but he is no sorcerer. On the contrary, I think him a good man. In any case, he is my friend, as you say, and I do not wish to hear you give him evil names."

"You do not wish it, your lordship? Very well, I will not say it. He is a good man, a saint, perhaps, or possibly an angel in disguise. Who knows? But what species of angel, eh? You are sure? You can tell? What did the curé say in his sermon last Sunday? I go to Mass, as you know, every Sunday, to confession also, at least once a year. But what did the curé say? Satan can deceive the saints even, when he puts on his best clothes. But not Jean Baptiste Giroux. Oh, no! Nobody could fool him, not even a woman, certainly not a poor old woman like me."

Mère Tabeau relapsed into silence, puffing at her black pipe, but steadily regarding Jean with her fish-like eyes. His curiosity was aroused.

"Madame Tabeau," he said, in a conciliating tone, "do not be angry. I was to blame. You may say what you please. You have something to tell me, and I will gladly listen."

"Oh, he will listen; his grandeur will deign to hear what the old woman has to say. But he will hear nothing."

"Madame Tabeau, I am a fool, as you have said, in effect, and I believe everybody. It is quite possible that I may be deceived, as on some former occasions. But you are a wise woman, Madame, and you know something. Will you not tell it to me for my advantage? I shall be grateful, even if you tell me what I do not wish to hear."

"Well, Jean, that is better. You have some sense left, in spite of your studies, a little intelligence still, strange to say. Sit down here on the step; no, not so far away; right here beside me. I will not hurt you, and the young ladies will not be jealous. Forty years ago they might have been annoyed, the vixens, but not now. Listen! There is a story, certainly. You shall hear it, no one else.

"At that time they did not call me Mère Tabeau. Bonhomme Tabeau, the old sot, had not yet come on the scene. He was rich, the old miser—that was why

I married him. Yes, and he died, as expected, in the course of a few years. But can you believe it? The old beast did not leave me one sou, not one sou—that was what I did not expect. All was for masses for his soul. The old fool! His soul is in the pit, where no masses can help him. I know theology, me. Masses can pull one out of purgatory, of course; but from the pit, never. Ah, that was one who got his deserts. His money goes to the priests, whom he did not love, and his soul remains with Satan. *Cru-ru-ru de Dieu!*"

"But it was of your friend the sorcerer that I was speaking. That was another who had sold himself to the evil one. At what price? Gold and the love of woman. Was he handsome? By no means. But how strong he was, how black his hair and his eyes! And how he would look at me and say: 'Angel, my angel, if you love me, if you love me truly, kiss me on both cheeks, and on the lips. Again! Once more!' And after that! *Mon Dieu*, after that his ship came in with the tide and he sailed away; while I, like a fool, stood on the shore and waved to him until he was out of sight beyond the point. And then I cried like a baby. Can you believe it?

"Did Michel Gamache not come back after the voyage? Ah, yes. When summer was gone he came back, but not to me. I was expecting him, I who had given him so much love; but he did not come that evening, nor the next, nor ever again. Always he was at the house of Bonhomme Duval, the rich trader, smuggler, thief. The old rascal had a daughter, of course. Beautiful? Not at all. It was the dowry that Michel desired. For that he perjured his soul, for the value of a hundred pounds, more or less. It was all arranged. The wedding was to take place on the first day of the year. They would begin the year together, those two. And I? They had no thought for me. Every evening I looked from the window, hoping that he would come, that he would wish to say good-bye, if nothing more; but I saw only the bare trees and the dead leaves dancing in the autumn wind.

"But listen, my friend. That is not the end of the story. No, only the beginning. My brother Ovide, do you know him? But how could you? He has been dead these thirty years. Since that night he was never the same man."

"What night, Madame?" said Jean, much interested.

"Be silent, fool!" said the old hag. "If you interrupt me again you may tell the story yourself. It was the eve of Christmas, of course, eight days before the wedding that was to be. The wedding! Ha! Ha! The sorcerer's wedding! He who had not made his Easter confession in seven years, he who had sold his soul for gold. His wedding! *Nom de diable!*

"'Sister,' said my brother Ovide, 'little sister, never mind; the wedding will never take place. I will kill him, the traitor.'

"'Kill him, yes, yes, kill him!' I said. 'But no, that would be too dangerous, for it is quite possible that he might kill you, Ovide, my brother. You are strong, I know, but not like him. Think of that neck of his, those hands, and that jaw, with teeth like a wolf. No, my brother, you shall not. I would kill him myself, but I fear—I don't know what I fear.'

"'Fear nothing, my sister, you shall see.'

"As I have said, it was still eight days before Christmas. No, two days only. Christmas was on a

Sunday that year, and it is Friday night that I speak of. I am not likely to forget it, nor the following night either. Michel used to visit the Duval place every evening at eight o'clock, returning always before midnight and going across the river to his home on the Island. The road was marked, as usual, by *balises*, for the path was always being effaced by the drifting snow. *Mon Dieu!* How the wind blew across the river, and how it carried the snow along—the snow that covered everything like a winding-sheet! Yes, and it would have covered Michel Gamache that night if my brother Ovide had had his way.

"Ah, he was a fox, that Ovide. He did not wish to meet Michel face to face, but to change the *balises* so that the road led direct to an air-hole, where the icy water ran along black and silent—that was not at all dangerous for him. If Michel should fall in the water, that was not his affair; but if he should try to climb out again, he would be there to push him down under the ice. Yes, under the ice, to drift, to roll along with the stream, to have his hair, his eyes, his ears, filled with slime, to have his bones picked by the eels, to be buried in a heap of sand and seaweed on some lonely shore—that would be a punishment indeed for Michel Gamache, liar, traitor, cursed sorcerer.

"So my brother Ovide hid himself behind one of the branches and waited. It was nearly midnight; the night was very cold; and Ovide was not at all comfortable as he crouched behind the little tree. But he warmed himself now and then from a flask of excellent brandy; soon his spirits rose, and he was full of courage. Presently he heard a light patter as of some one running with moccasins on his feet; and immediately there appeared, not a man, but a gigantic wolf, that stopped at the open water, and began to howl as though scenting danger. Then he took a leap into the air, flying over an abyss of twenty feet, lit on the ice on the other side, and disappeared in the distance, still howling frightfully.

"My brother Ovide escaped from that place as fast as possible, believing himself chased by the devil; and when he staggered into the house, his face pale as the snow, his jaw hanging, his eyes bloodshot and staring, he was not a courageous object, I assure you.

"'What is the matter, Ovide,' said I, much frightened.

"'Lock the door, Celestine; it is following me. Quick, it is there.'

"'What is it, you fool?' said I.

"'The *loup garou*, Celestine! Ah! Ah! There it is at the window! *Mon Dieu! Mon Dieu!*'

"Ovide fell in a heap on the floor, still pointing with trembling finger at the window, and there I saw, I, Celestine Colomb, the flaming eyes of some ferocious beast. It was terrifying. 'Jesus-Maria!' I cried, making the holy sign, and saying all my prayers at once. The apparition vanished, but I could not forget the fearful eyes, and all night long I was seeing them in my dreams.

"On the next day, at half-past two in the afternoon, I put on my best dress and my French shoes, and went to visit Annette Duval.

"'Annette,' I said, as politely as possible, 'you do not love me, perhaps; and I, possibly, do not love you.'

"'Perhaps not,' said Annette, beginning to cry, 'but I do not hate you, Celestine. I pray for you, even.'

"'That is not necessary, Annette,' said I, with scorn.

'I can make my salvation myself, thank you. I do not love you, as I have said, but I would not have you marry a sorcerer.'

"'What is that you say? A sorcerer? Michel a sorcerer? Nonsense! If you had nothing better to say why did you come?'

"'I came, Annette, to say that Michel is a sorcerer, one who has not made his Easter confession in seven years, one who has sold his soul to the devil. Not only so, but he becomes a *loup garou* every evening at midnight. My brother Ovide has seen him change into a *loup garou* only last night.'

"'Mademoiselle,' said Annette, becoming very pale, 'be so kind as to go away.'

"'Annette,' said I, 'listen to me. Ask him why he leaves you every evening before midnight. Ask him to stay with you for a few minutes longer, and you will see.'

"'Mademoiselle Colomb,' said Annette, rising, 'permit me to show you the door.'

"This time I went without a word. It was not necessary to say more. Annette was troubled, and would certainly ask Michel for an explanation. And so it turned out.

"Some time before midnight, Ovide and I—Ovide would not go alone—hid ourselves in the bushes near the door of Bonhomme Duval, the door which Annette had shown to me, not once only, but twice. But I was to show her something; I, Celestine Colomb. Ovide had his gun loaded with a silver bullet, a bullet which I had made with my own hands—for the sorcerer, of course. Ovide had a knife also, long and sharp. Michel does not forget that knife, I think.

"It lacked but a few minutes of midnight when the door opened and there stood Michel and Annette on the threshold in the light of the fire. Annette was angry, as we could see; and Michel, that giant who could have strangled her with one hand, was trying to pacify her, to explain what could not be explained.

"'So,' she said, 'you must go, it seems, although I have prayed you to stay a few minutes longer, to spend the first moments of Christmas with me—and you will not.'

"'Annette, my dear Annette, have I not said that I must go? It is an important appointment.'

"'Important? Oh yes, more important than I, of course. I see. You do not love me. No, it is money that you love, that only.'

"'Not at all, Annette, it is that I must meet a friend.'

"'A friend, Michel! What kind of a friend?'

"'Annette, I cannot tell you. It is a matter of life and death. I must go. Good-bye, dear. A kiss, a single kiss.'

"'No, no! Never again! Ah, can I believe it? It is true, then, what Celestine has said. You are a sorcerer, and your friend, your friend, Michel, is Satan. *Mon Dieu! Mon Dieu!*'

"At this word Michel began to laugh, but presently the laugh became very strange, more like the cry of a wild animal than the voice of a man; he began to lose the human shape; his coat became the skin of a beast; his feet and hands became paws; long ears grew upon his head; the jaw was thrust forth and the fangs protruded. *Nom de Dieu!* It was a wolf, a *loup garou*, that, with a ferocious growl, precipitated itself upon Annette, who fell unconscious on the ground.

THE LOUP GAROU

"'Shoot, shoot, Ovide!' I screamed, but Ovide, stupefied by terror, stood there groaning and muttering.

"'It is he! It is he! The *loup garou!* Child of the devil! He will destroy me, body and soul! It is he! It is he! *Mon Dieu! Mon Dieu!*'

"Hearing this, the wolf left Annette and rushed upon us. Then the courage of Ovide returned; he seized the gun and aimed a terrible blow at the head of the beast. But this ferocious animal, evading the blow, in an instant was at my brother's throat. In another minute Ovide would have been in Hell. It was I who saved him; I who came to the rescue with the long knife; I who struck the blow that should have killed the *loup garou*. By an unlucky chance the blade missed the neck but cut off half of the ear. It drew blood, of course; the beast changed instantly into the human form; and there stood the traitor, Michel Gamache; his face streaming with blood; and there on the snow lay, not the ear of a wolf, but that of a man. Would you like to see it, Jean Baptiste? There it is! I keep it with me all the time, as a souvenir.

"The wedding—did it take place? Certainly not! Annette would have married the sorcerer in spite of all, but her people would not hear of it. Now she is 'Sister Sainte Anne' in the Convent of the Ursulines, where she prays all the time for the soul of the sorcerer. Does she pray also for her dear friend, Celestine Colomb? As to that, you may ask the sorcerer. Go! Ask him, too, why he has lost his ear."

"Good evening, Jean," said Michel Gamache, a little later. "You have been delayed, but no matter. There remains an hour of twilight and there will be a clear moon to-night. You have been talking to that she-devil, Mère Tabeau, I see."

"*Mon Dieu!* Monsieur Gamache, how do you know that?" said Jean, astonished.

"Oh, my friend, I see many things," said the sorcerer, showing his teeth and uttering a weird laugh. "So you have been making friends with La Colomb. Fine company for a young man. And did she tell you that I was a *loup garou*, and that she cut off a piece of my ear—hein?"

"*Sacré*, Monsieur Gamache, that is just what she said. But I did not believe a word of it."

"Oh, believe it if you like, Jean, until I give you another version of the story. But regard my ear. Does it look as though it had been sliced with a knife?"

"No, Monsieur Gamache, not at all. Quite otherwise."

"Quite otherwise, I assure you," said the sorcerer, with a ferocious smile. "Listen! she saved the life of that precious brother, Ovide, and my ear—*sacré tonnerre!*—she bit it off!"

CHAPTER V

CASTLES IN SPAIN

It was the morning of the twenty-fourth of June, and Jean Baptiste, having attended Mass in honour of his patron saint, was spending the rest of the day by the river. The sun was high, and in all open places the heat was intense, but where Jean lay at ease near the edge of a cliff there was cool and pleasant shade. At his feet the river roared through a deep gorge; on the farther side there was a wall of rock with a fringe of trees; while beyond rose a long range of mountains, forest-clad to the very top. Above, in the blue, floated light, silvery clouds, lazily passing from tree-top to tree-top, slowly changing their form, until they disappeared behind the mountains or melted away in the depths of the sky.

On this day Jean was celebrating his twenty-third birthday, and the completion of his college course. His college had been the forest, and his book the book of Nature. He had read other books as well; all that the seminarists had studied, and many more of which they had never heard; but the knowledge that he valued most was obtained from the trees, the rocks, the soil, the river, the birds, the beasts, the fishes, the cycle of the seasons, the changes of the weather, and all the panorama and procession of Nature that mean so much to the man with the seeing eye and the understanding heart. The book was always open; and in the light of Science, with Philosophy his interpreter and Religion his inspiration, he read many difficult pages and discovered many secrets.

To Jean Baptiste the study of the world in which he lived afforded not merely satisfaction to the natural curiosity of youth, which makes knowledge desirable for itself alone; but it gave him an insight into the nature of things, and a power of control which he planned to use, some day, for a higher end. The savages, by their knowledge of the wilderness, had made their living there; the habitants, knowing more, had secured many of the comforts of civilised life; and it was reasonable to think that a fuller knowledge would yield results undreamed of by those who never went below the surface of things to the centre and source of power.

Since the time when he decided that he would not be a priest, a religious leader of the conventional type, Jean had become possessed with the thought that there was another work to which he was called, a work more material in its character, but none the less for the good of the parish, the honour of his patron saint and the glory of God. Of that he had been thinking for many years; for that he had been preparing; and now the day was at hand and the work about to begin.

Jean had many plans for the improvement of his little world, not the least of which was the using of the river itself, an enormous source of power going to waste in its mad rush through the gorge at his feet. Looking up stream he could see, not a hundred yards distant, the deep, still pool where the cataract began; and beyond, on both sides of the river, a broad expanse of low-lying ground, stretching to the first rise of hills and forming a perfect site for a dam and an immense lake which should afford water-power equal to the strength of ten thousand horses.

With such energy at his command, what could he not do? Carry on lumbering on a large scale, work the great deposits of iron sand along the river, manufacture pottery out of the banks of fine clay, run a tramway to Quebec, light and heat all the houses in the parish with electricity, supply the people with motive power for machinery of every kind—all this and more was possible. As he thought of the wonderful possibilities it seemed to Jean Baptiste that he was a prophet, the fore-runner of a mighty revolution in this remote valley, where for a hundred years the habitants had desired nothing else than to walk in peace and security in the ways of their fathers.

But it was not possible to leave them in peace. No, the new age was come. Quebec and Montreal, Lorette and Chaudière were advancing by leaps and bounds, and the habitants of St. Placide must arise and join the procession. Consider that fine river, the St. Ange, rising in a hundred lakes on the height of land and descending in a thousand cataracts to its final plunge into the St. Lawrence. Why had the good God given this gift if not for use, that the people might be more industrious, more prosperous and more happy in their little corner of the great and beautiful world?

True, it would be necessary to have capital for the beginning of any of these enterprises, and that was the chief hindrance in the way of the realization of Jean's dreams. He had no property of his own; and his mother's farm, with houses, barns, cattle, horses and all, was worth only a few thousand dollars. There were two or three rich habitants in the parish, like M. Taché and M. Laroche, but would they be willing to risk their hard-earned wealth in the launching of schemes that must seem to them visionary and impracticable? There was great wealth among the merchants and bankers of Quebec, but how the owners of it could be induced to embark in the enterprise was a problem that Jean, with all his learning, had not been able to solve.

He had not yet worked out the financial details, but if only he could make a beginning, everything else would come in the course of time. "It is the first step that costs," says the proverb, and Jean was determined to take that step at any cost. After that he would take the second, the third and all the other steps, until he arrived at the summit of his ambition.

The summit—what was that? When one arrived at the summit of yonder mountain that seemed to touch the clouds, there was a higher peak beyond; and when one came to that elevation there was a peak still higher, until in the end one stood upon the height of land that divides the waters flowing South into the St. Lawrence from those that go North and East into the abyss of the Saguenay. Then one could rest, perhaps, unless one wished to explore and climb other peaks, beyond the Saguenay and Lake St. John, or in distant lands. But it was not necessary to go so far, for there was great satisfaction to be had in climbing for the mere love of the sport, even if one did not reach the top of everything.

At least, Jean would be a great man in the parish, greater than M. Taché, as great, almost, as the curé himself, and that was something. M. Paradis would always be the spiritual power, but Jean would be the temporal power, like the Pope and the Emperor of former times, and they would work together in perfect harmony for the good of the parish. Jean had no desire to be Pope, but Emperor he would be—Emperor of St. Placide, the Emperor Jean Baptiste.

Jean laughed at the absurdity of his day-dream—but was it so absurd after all? What is the world but a collection of empires; and what is an empire but a number of parishes? Why could not the great man of a parish be as happy as an emperor, as the lord of a world? If he had congenial work, free scope for his activities, wealth sufficient for the simple wants, a good name in the parish, and a few loving friends—what more could he desire? What more could he ask of the good God?

Yet there was one thing that he had forgotten, although he had been thinking of it all the time. When one was building castles in Spain how could one forget the châtelaine? What was the use of a castle, of riches, of a great name, with nobody to share one's happiness? It would be too lonely, too discouraging. Yes, there must be a châtelaine, a tall, lovely lady with dark-blue eyes and golden hair—no, not just golden, but of a ruddy tinge like a sunrise cloud, bronze-coloured with a glint of gold. It would be bound with a fillet of blue and would fall in wavy iridescent masses down her back. She would be clad in a long garment of purple velvet with a border of golden braid and a golden girdle about her waist.

"But yes," said Jean to himself, "there must be a châtelaine, but what is her name? *Mon Dieu*, what is her name?"

"*Mon Dieu*, what is her name? I should very much

like to know," said a laughing voice behind the trees. "Will you not tell me her name, where you have met her, what she is like, and all that? I am dying to know."

Startled and speechless, Jean turned suddenly, and from behind the trees came tripping an apparition the like of which had surely never before been seen on the banks of the St. Ange. It was tall for a girl, a lithe, graceful figure clad in fishing costume, with small rubber boots, a short skirt of brown cotton, a waist and jacket of the same material, and a jaunty cap set above a mass of reddish-golden hair. There were dark-blue eyes, almost black, dancing with merriment, a laughing mouth set with pearly teeth, a dimpled chin and a dainty nose, the least bit retroussé. The vision carried a light rod in her hand and a pannier slung across her shoulder. She advanced rapidly, as though expecting a joyous greeting, but suddenly stopped, poised as though for flight, and said, with an injured air:

"So, Jean, you have forgotten me. You don't know your old friends any more. Well, I will leave you; I will go down to the river and catch another fish. Good-bye, Monsieur the Hermit, I leave you to your meditations."

"Don't go, Gabrielle!" exclaimed Jean, quite alarmed. "I know you very well, although I have seen you only once or twice in seven years. But how you have changed! You are much better looking than formerly."

"Oh, thank you, Monsieur Giroux. From you that is a compliment indeed. What an ugly little beast I must have been!"

"No, Gabrielle, not at all. On the contrary, you

were always charming, but now you are enchanting, of a beauty altogether——"

"Stop, stop, Jean. That is enough. I am not used to such talk. At the convent it is not permitted, and when one sees the young men of Quebec, which is not often, they do not dare. What would the Mother Superior say, or Sister Ste. Marthe? No, you must not. You are impertinent, yes, impertinent, I say."

"No, Gabrielle, not that; only an old friend. But tell me, how many fish have you caught?"

"Three, Jean, three beauties. Look!"

As Jean bent down to look into the open basket, it was not of the trout that he was thinking, but of the lovely fisherwoman by his side, whose golden head was so close to his own, and whose rosy cheek he would so much like to kiss. Yes, he would like to take her in his arms and bestow a kiss upon those laughing lips and those dancing eyes. Truly—and the thought came to him like a flash of lightning—this was the châtelaine of his castle in Spain, the golden lady of his dreams.

"Well," said Gabrielle, with a provoking smile that made an alluring dimple in her cheek, "have you lost your tongue, or is it another meditation that you have begun, Monsieur the Hermit? But tell me what you think of my fish? I caught them myself—will you believe it?—and with this fly. See! Queen of the Waters."

"Queen of the Waters," repeated Jean. "What a lovely creature! A sort of water nymph, with golden hair, blue eyes like the sky, a brown dress and rubber boots. *Mon Dieu!* What boots for a water nymph!"

Gabrielle shut the basket with a snap.

"Stupid!" she said. "I will not talk to you. You have lost your head."

"Yes, Gabrielle, that is it. Lost, absolutely, and my heart as well."

"Your heart, Jean, that is interesting. I did not know that you had a heart. And you have lost it? What a pity! Who has found it, I wonder? Who has it? What is her name? *Mon Dieu*, what is her name?"

"Gabrielle!"

"Well, go on, confess. It will do you good. You need it."

"True," said Jean, very seriously. "That is just what I have done, and to you. Her name, it is Gabrielle. Do you, can you understand?"

Gabrielle grew pale.

"That will do, Jean. That goes too far. I will not allow jests of that sort. Good-bye. I must go home now to cook these trout for dinner."

"But it is no jest—far from it. I love you, Gabrielle, to distraction; more than I can tell. Could you not——?"

"No, Monsieur Giroux, I could not. And I beg of you never to speak to me like that again."

"But why, Gabrielle, what reason?"

"Do you wish to know, Monsieur Giroux? Do you really wish to know?"

"Yes, certainly, Mademoiselle Taché."

"Then you shall have it. Do you know what the neighbours say, what my father says, what I say? It is that you are a good-for-nothing, Jean Baptiste Giroux. Do you understand? A good-for-nothing! There, I have said it, and it is true."

" Is that all, Gabrielle ? " said Jean, in a steady voice.

" All ? " exclaimed Gabrielle, turning on him in a blaze of anger. " All ? *Mon Dieu!* It is enough, I should think."

With that she went away up the path, carrying her head very high, never once looking back to see the effect of this last crushing blow.

But, strange to say, Jean did not seem to be crushed.

" Well, that was brave of me," he said to himself. " I did not think I could do it. I am rejected, of course, and in despair. ' Good-for-nothing ! ' That is bad, but it is a defect that may be corrected. If that were all ! Ah, if that were all ! But what a vision of loveliness ! What spirit ! What courage ! Gabrielle ! Name of an Angel ! Now at last I know her name. It is she, no other."

CHAPTER VI

THE HABITANT

AFTER what had happened Jean could not ask Monsieur Taché for help in his great enterprise. He therefore applied to Monsieur Laroche, the only other rich man in the parish, and was received with scorn.

"So," said Bonhomme Laroche, "you wish to build a dam across the St. Ange, to inundate the best land on your mother's farm, to make a pond for ducks. A great work, truly! And I am to lend you a small sum of money — ten thousand dollars, only. Why not ask for a hundred thousand? That would be nothing at all for me—a mere bagatelle. We are rich, we habitants of St. Placide, men of high finance, millionaires, and we love to encourage hare-brained enthusiasts by small loans. And on what security? A dam of logs that the first spring flood will take away. You are a fool, a dam fool. Ha! Ha! Yes, a dam fool. My little joke, you see.

"But, Jean, do not go, do not be angry at my little pleasantry. I have yet a piece of advice which I will give you for nothing, although it will be worth much to you if you have the sense to take it. Listen! You have a good farm; that is to say, your mother has it, which is the same thing, since all your brothers and sisters, the whole tribe, have gone away. Go home, Jean, to the farm; raise hay, potatoes, cattle, pigs, chickens—all that. Be an honest cultivator, like your fathers for many generations. It was good enough for them; it will be good enough for you. You will wish to make some improvements, no doubt—a new barn, a stable, a house, possibly. Good! I might be able to lend you a small sum, a thousand dollars, perhaps, or even two thousand, if necessary. The rate of interest? What is that between friends? We will arrange all that.

"Now, Jean," and here the old man assumed a confidential air, " to be a good habitant one must have a good wife. Do not blush, my lad, it is only a matter of business. Without that no habitant can succeed. One's marriage should help one along, should it not? Assuredly. That goes without saying. Well, there is my daughter Blanchette, for example. I do not say that she is very young, nor more beautiful than others, but how capable, how accomplished! And she will have a dowry, of course, something generous, you may be sure. All the other children are well provided for, and I am not yet a pauper, no indeed. There. I have said it. Consider it well, at your leisure. There is no haste to decide. I will see your mother and all can be arranged without embarrassment. *Au revoir*, Jean. Come to see us when you can."

Jean did not like the advice of Bonhomme Laroche, but part of it, at least, he was obliged to take, for there was no alternative, and at sunrise on the following day he was in the fields with the hired man, dexterously swinging a long scythe and laying low great swathes of timothy and red clover. He was in perfect physical condition, with every nerve and muscle surging with energy, so that the work did not tire him, but only served to release the pent-up emotion of his soul. For the soul of Jean Baptiste was full of wrath, and as he gripped the handles of the scythe and swung the keen blade through the grass with a venomous hiss, he seemed to be cutting down an army of enemies and mercilessly trampling them underfoot.

The neighbours, those ignorant, spiteful people with their vicious gossip—how he despised them all! They hated to see a person rise above them in the slightest degree, and were always reaching out envious hands to pull him down. They wanted to make a habitant of him? Well, a habitant he would be, and beat them at their own game. Of what good was all his education if he could not use it in the growing of potatoes and the raising of pigs? Yes, pigs. The neighbours were well satisfied with a yearling hog that weighed a hundred and fifty pounds, when it might as well be two hundred pounds or three hundred even. It was a question of breed and care, as it was with cattle, horses, sheep, fowl, and every other animal on the farm. As to chickens, for example, they laid eggs in plenty all summer, at fifteen cents a dozen, but laid none at all in winter when the price rose to sixty cents and more. Why such stupidity? A question of management, merely, of knowledge and attention to business. In fact, the more Jean thought of habitant life the greater seemed the possibilities of improvement in every direction. Besides, it was a life not to be despised, that of a successful cultivator, the happiest, most independent man on earth.

Certainly the advice of Bonhomme Laroche was not to be despised. But borrow money from the old miser he would not, nor marry his daughter Blanchette if she were as beautiful as an angel from Heaven. The dowry ? Did the old miser think that he could buy the hearts, the souls of men ? Who would barter love for gold ? Who would give that which was beyond all price for all the land, the barns, the cattle of the parish —of the world ? Yet there were those who would gladly make such an exchange, the poor, deluded fools.

As to Gabrielle, that was different. There was a girl of a beauty most rare, with her tall, lithe figure, her springing step, her dainty little head with its wealth of golden hair, those laughing eyes like the depths of the sky, that tantalizing, alluring smile. It was as though an angel had descended to earth to show to mortal man the perfection of beauty of the heavenly world. But what pride, what scorn, what contempt ! And how unfair, how cruel ! Not a thought of justice, not a word of excuse, no chance to explain. Mademoiselle Taché was too far above Jean Baptiste Giroux. In what way ? In intellect ? By no means. In education ? Not at all. In manners ? Far from it. In wealth ? Ah, that was it, the pride of purse, the base contempt for all merit that had not the stamp of gold. " Good-for-nothing ! *Sacrée petite vierge !* "

But wait—a year, two years, three at most—and he would show the little vixen whom it was that she had attacked with an insult so contemptible, so injurious. Then, when she would be only too glad to receive the attentions of the chief man in the parish, he would turn away and devote himself to another. But what other ? Blanchette Laroche ? Not for a thousand dowries. Who then ? Well, there would be time enough to arrange that little detail. There were still good fish in the sea, though scarce and very wary. But in any case it would be necessary to humble the pride of that scornful beauty. " Good-for-nothing! *Sacrés mille tonnerres!*"

Jean was certainly in an unhappy state of mind. Of all the neighbours he could not think of one who was his friend. Not Mère Tabeau, certainly; that old witch with the bleared eyes and the yellow teeth. She liked to talk with him now and then, but only to spit out venom. Not Michel Gamache, who was not to be trusted, a sorcerer, and no friend of man. Not Father Paradis, even; that good old priest who had been for so many years his teacher, his Mentor. Not even he, for he was disappointed in Jean because he had not taken up some useful work. Even his mother had lost faith in him. Had he not seen her looking at him with wistful, sorrowful eyes, because he was not fulfilling the promise of his early years? She also was against him, and he would have to fight the battle alone. Give it up? No, with the help of God and Saint Jean he would do battle to the very end, and would show them all what it was to fight and to win.

Thus Jean, as he toiled in the field, under the hot sun, poured forth all the bitterness of his soul, until the bitterness was gone, the wrath evaporated, and the strong man began to rejoice once more in the work of his hands. At high noon he sat down in the shade of a moss-covered rock, beside a bubbling spring, and ate the dinner that his mother had provided with gladness of heart. Never had bread and butter tasted so sweet, with fresh eggs, tasty sausage, and the jam of wild strawberries that the good mother had made with her own hands. It was an excellent meal, nourishing to body and soul; and when, after an hour's rest in the cool shade, Jean resumed his work, refreshed and strengthened, the troubles that had come into his life took their proper place in the order and scheme of things, not as incurable evils but as obstacles to be overcome by unswerving determination and persistent effort.

So Jean wrought hard all through the long day, doing the work of two men; and when, after sunet, he hung his scythe in the crook of a tree and began to climb the long hill toward home, he had put his troubles behind his back, and set his face toward the future with strong courage and a spirit of charity toward all mankind.

The life of a habitant, he thought, was not all hardship. There was work, to be sure, plenty of it; but what was that to a strong man? There was little money to be had, but one had all the necessaries of life and some of the luxuries as well. At night, how one could sleep, and in the morning how one arose with a rested body and a cheerful heart!

The neighbours? They were true friends, after all, kind-hearted, well-meaning, with all their little gossip, and their advice was good, excellent. One must have a footing in the world, else how could one accomplish anything? One must take the first step before one takes the second. One must humble oneself in the day of small things, and bide one's time, if one was to be ready when the great opportunity came which only a man of experience could seize and control. Sooner or later he would win, for the dice were loaded in his favour; but win or lose it was a great thing to live and to bear a part in the interesting and wonderful world, where every morning was a new day and every evening a new surprise.

CHAPTER VII

HER MAJESTY'S MAIL

"Ah, there you are at last," said Madame Giroux, who was lighting the lamp for the evening meal as Jean entered. "You have worked hard to-day, my son. At this rate the hay will soon be cut, will it not? But sit down and take your soup, while I tell you something.

"You knew, of course, that Tom Sullivan was likely to lose the mail contract. Well, he has lost it, or will lose it very soon, as you will see from this paper which Monsieur Laroche has given me. It is whisky again, it seems. As Monsieur Laroche says, the good Canadians can drink in moderation, but the Irish do not know when to stop. For me, I would have them all stop before they begin. What a waste of good money! And to lose the mail contract as well—what folly! But listen:

"'MAIL CONTRACT.

"'Sealed applications addressed to the Minister of Posts will be received at Ottawa up to noon of Wednesday, the first of July, 1899, for carrying Her Majesty's Mails under the conditions of a contract covering a term of four years, twice a week, going and returning, between Quebec and St. Placide, to commence on the fifteenth of July following.'

" There, Jean, what do you think of that ? "

" It is an opportunity," said Jean, " and I will make application at once ; but I wish that it had not been suggested by Bonhomme Laroche."

" Why not, Jean ? He is a rich man, and has influence with the Government. He will help you, I am sure, if you ask him to do so."

" I will not ask him, my mother, but I think that I shall win just the same. The Irish have had the contract for some years, and it is our turn now. Tom received a hundred dollars, did he not ? One dollar for a drive of thirty miles, regardless of the weather. The Government is not liberal, certainly ; but there will be passengers to carry now and then, and I can take butter and eggs to market in Quebec, where I shall receive better prices than at Beauport. Oh, I can see a clear profit of two hundred dollars a year, at the very least. My mother, we shall soon be as rich as Bonhomme Laroche, the old miser. Yes, I will apply to-morrow morning. There will be other applicants, no doubt."

" Yes, Jean. Tom's cousin, Paddy Brady, will try for it, to keep it in the family, you see."

" That begins to be interesting," said Jean, with a smile. " A little conflict of races, it seems. The Irish settlement will be up in arms."

" Yes, Jean, and I am afraid of Tom Sullivan. He is big and strong and has a terrible temper, I am told. He might do you harm, Jean."

" Do not fear, my mother. We have a good understanding, Tom and I, for we have had some little affairs already, you see. No, there is no danger at all. Well, in three weeks I shall be carrying Her Majesty's Mails.

That is not the summit of my ambition, by any means, but it is a step. Who can tell to what it may lead ?"

On the very next day Jean sent his application to headquarters in Ottawa, and in about ten days received official notice of his appointment. At the same time Tom Sullivan and Paddy Brady heard the news, and their expressions of rage can better be imagined than described. They exhausted the resources of the English language in cursing Jean Baptiste and all his ancestors, and uttered imprecations in the old Erse tongue that were fearsome to hear. The bystanders were alarmed, and came to Jean to urge him to surrender the contract if he wished to save his life.

But Jean was not to be deterred from his purpose by any threats, and before dawn on the fifteenth of July he took the road for Quebec in his spring cart, with the light mail-bag under the seat and a supply of butter and eggs for the Champlain market. He was in high spirits, for all his work was going well, and he was making a fair start along the road to success. The years of preparation were over, and he was beginning to carry out his plans, to realize his dreams. The time of deliberation was at an end; the time for action had begun.

The morning was dark, but as Jean drove along the road the sky brightened, the stars went out one by one, and a rosy glow appeared in the East, chasing the shadows down the mountain-side, until the whole valley was filled with the clear light of day. As he reached the summit of the last hill he saw the sun rise over the mountains of Notre Dame. It touched all the circle of the hills with a tinge of gold, gleamed on the tin roofs and spires of Quebec, illuminated the slopes of Beauport, the Isle of Orleans and the cliffs of Levis, while the great river shone like burnished silver, and the ships, with their white sails, moved up stream with the rising tide. The heart of Jean Baptiste rose to greet the rising sun; his soul exulted in the glorious view; and his strong voice broke into song as he descended the long slope that led to the historic Beauport Road.

> " A Saint-Malo beau port de mer,
> A Saint-Malo, beau port de mer,
> Trois gros navir's sout arrivés.
> Nous irons sur l'eau
> Nous y prom' promener
> Nous irons jouer dans l'île.
>
> " Trois gros navir's sont arrivés,
> Trois gros navir's sont arrivés,
> Chargés d'avoin', chargés de bled.
> Nous irons sur l'eau
> Nous y prom' promener,
> Nous irons jouer dans l'île."

Jean sang the dear, foolish old song to the very end, and sang it again and again until he came to the main road and joined the stream of vehicles of every description that were carrying hay and grain, butter and eggs, potatoes and onions, strawberries and currants, and all the produce of the Côte de Beaupré to the markets of Quebec. He was not well known in those parts, but had a cheerful greeting for all as he passed, and by the time he reached the bridge over the St. Charles it was known to half of the inhabitants of Beauport and many people from the more distant parishes that there was a new mail carrier from St. Placide, a gay, dare-devil of a fellow, a reckless driver, but withal a young man whom it was a pleasure to meet along the way, so debonair, so joyous, a good fellow in every sense of the word. There were those, even, who knew his name, who remembered his father, pronounced him a chip of the old block, and prophesied for him a brilliant career if he did not break his neck before he got well started on the road to fame and fortune.

In the afternoon, as Jean was returning by the same road, he was not so cheerful, and he did not sing, for the day had not fulfilled the promise of the morning hours. Soon after he crossed the toll bridge his horse cast a shoe, and he was obliged to return to a blacksmith's shop in the city, where he spent an hour of his time and a considerable part of his day's wages. Besides, he had to pay another toll at the bridge, which was irritating. A little later, as he was driving along at a rapid pace, trying to make up for lost time, a wheel came off the cart, and he narrowly escaped a bad fall. There was another hour's delay, and further expense.

Jean's reflections, as he toiled up the long, sandy hill toward the mountains, were anything but agreeable. He had given a whole day's work for nothing and less than nothing. He would arrive late with the mail, receive a reprimand from the postmaster, and hear the sneering remarks of the impatient neighbours. Worst of all, he had been outwitted by Tom and Paddy, for there could be little doubt that both accidents had been brought about by some trickery of theirs, and it was impossible to tell what they would do next. Certainly, there was less profit in the contract than he had thought, and little prospect of improvement; but give it up because of opposition he would not, not if all the Sullivans and Bradys of the Irish settlement were to set upon him.

The sun was sinking behind the mountain as Jean

reached the summit of the long hill, and it was almost dark when he came to the "Forks," about a mile from the first house. The main road led direct to St. Placide, about five miles away, while the road to the left went up over the mountain in the direction of Lake Beauport, and reached St. Placide by a route circuitous and difficult, especially after dark. Jean's horse was accustomed to the main road, but stopped at the " Forks," and then quickly turned to climb the hill on the left.

" *Sacré fou de cheval*," said Jean, with a laugh, " where are you going? You are not hungry, then. You don't want to get home before midnight. There now, come about. It was a mistake. This way, old fellow. *Marche donc!* "

The horse came about, though unwillingly, but just as he had begun to trot along in response to a sharp cut of the whip, Jean heard a voice that seemed to come from some one standing directly in front of him :

" Take the other road ! "

" Who's there ? " said Jean, looking to see who could be on the lonely road so late in the evening, but was surprised to find that nobody was in sight, while the horse began to rear and to back in sheer terror, and nearly upset the cart.

" There now, there now, old fool," said Jean, in a reassuring voice. " You thought you heard something, did you? But nothing is there. Gently, now. It is nothing. Go on, then. We could go by the mountain, to be sure, but when should we arrive? No, my friend, we must take the usual way. Go along, now, softly, if you like, but go along. There is nothing to fear. Go along."

Jean drove on, in some little trepidation, it must be

confessed, and was not a little relieved when he heard the familiar sound of chopping, some distance ahead. Turning a corner he saw, about a hundred yards away, a man in the act of felling a large tree.

"Holloa, there!" he called. "Don't fell that tree. It will block the road. Don't fell it, I say! Ah, you idiot, you did it. Now, stupid, will you tell me how I shall get home."

"You can walk, damn you!" said Tom Sullivan, for it was he; and beside him stood his cousin, Paddy Brady, also with an axe in his hand.

"Oh, it is you, Tom," said Jean, with a friendly smile. "You are cutting some firewood, I see. Will you please take it out of the way as soon as possible."

"Take it away yourself, you damned Frenchman," said Tom, with a sneer. "What business have you coming along at this time o' night? A fine mail driver you are. You should have been at the office two hours ago. By the powers, it'll take you two hours more to get there on shank's mare. Ha! Ha! The new driver will be late, and it's not long he'll be carrying Her Majesty's Mail. Her Majesty'll be getting rid of him damn quick, I be thinking."

"Tom," said Jean, in a conciliatory but firm tone, "will you take that timber away, or will you not?"

"I will not," said Tom, defiantly.

"Then, Tom," said Jean, getting out of the cart and advancing deliberately, "will you lend me your axe for a minute?"

"Lend you my axe, you damned thief!" roared Tom, with a volley of curses. "I'll lend it to you. Yes! Take that!"

At the word Tom aimed a blow at Jean that would

have split his head open, but that he, stepping nimbly aside, let the axe swing harmlessly by, and before Tom could recover, closed with him, wrenched the weapon from his hands and flung him violently to the ground.

"Help, Paddy, help!" yelled Tom. "Kill him, Paddy! For the love of God, kill him, I say!"

But Paddy had no stomach for a fight, and stood aside with mingled amazement and admiration as Jean, turning his back on both his enemies, began to cut the branches of the tree, close to the bark, with great rapidity, until finally he cut away the top and only the bare trunk remained to block the way.

"Now, Paddy," said Jean, throwing down the axe, "if you will help me we'll throw this log out of the way. There, take hold of that end. Now, Paddy, heave!"

Paddy put forth all his strength, but could not lift the end of the log, while Jean lifted his end about three feet, and then let it drop.

"What's the matter, Paddy? Why don't you lift?"

"Cut it in two and I'll lift my end," said Paddy. "Why, man, it weighs a ton at the very least."

"A ton, Paddy, is that all? We can lift it, then. Come—another try."

"Not for me," said Paddy, standing back. "I know what I can do."

"Well," said Jean, "you surprise me, Paddy Brady. I am disappointed in you. But the log must go. Saint Jean to my aid. Watch me, Paddy."

With that Jean bent down, his arms between his knees, his fingers gripping the log like a vice, and as he rose the log rose, slowly, steadily, until Jean stood erect holding the great trunk in his iron grip. Taking a long breath he put forth a mighty effort and lifted the log by the strength of his arms alone, inch by inch, until it reached the height of a man and rested for a moment on his shoulder. Then, taking hold lower down, Jean raised the log with ease until it stood upright, when, with a slight push, he sent it crashing down the cliff to the rocks below.

"My God!" said Paddy, with a gasp. "What a lift! I feel as though all my bones were cracked. Jean Baptiste, my bully boy, it's the strong man of the world you are. Give me your hand, man alive. From now on I'm your friend, and it's sorry I am for what has happened. Forgive me, Jean, and Tom too. He meant you no harm."

"Say nothing, Paddy," said Jean, with a smile. "I am well content to have a friend like you. But your cousin—I fear that I have hurt him. Tom, my friend, I was too rough and I am sorry. Forgive me."

Tom Sullivan made no reply, but glared at his enemy like a wounded bear.

"Tom," persisted Jean, "will you not let me drive you home? As to the contract, you shall have it. I will give it up."

"Give it up, you damned thief? Yes, when I kill you. Forgive you? Yes, when you are in Hell!"

"But, Tom——"

"The curse o' Crummle on you!" snarled Tom, turning his face away in bitterness of soul.

CHAPTER VIII

THE CITY MAN

IT was a midsummer evening soon after Jean's first experience as mail-carrier, when he drove up to the house with a passenger, the first of a long procession of summer tourists that were to be the beginnings of prosperity to St. Placide.

"*Dieu merci!*" said the City Man, as the spring cart stopped at the Giroux door. "God be thanked that we are here at last! Let us descend. Ah, but I have cramps in my legs. What a drive! Four hours over those infernal roads, up and down those everlasting hills. But in the end we arrive; as the evening shadows fall we come to our destination. Behold a house in the wilderness. Regard the light in the window. See, the door opens and Madame the hostess appears on the threshold. Are we invited to enter?"

"Certainly," said Jean. "Come in, Monsieur. Let me present you to my mother, Monsieur, who will take care of you while I put my horse in the stable. My mother, this is Monsieur Trudel, a gentleman from Quebec who wishes to have a day's fishing in the St. Ange."

"Come in, Monsieur," said Madame Giroux, with a smile of welcome. "It is but a poor house, but we will give you of our best. See, you were expected, and the supper is on the table. Take a place, Monsieur; we will serve you immediately."

"With great pleasure, Madame. Ah, how good it is to have arrived somewhere! This is not the Hotel St. Louis, to be sure, nor even the Chien d'Or, but it is a comfortable habitant home, very proper in every way, as one sees. What a fine, solid old table! How cosy those rag carpets! How gay the blue china on the dresser—genuine willow pattern, too! How cheery that bright fire! It was getting cold outside. Ah, Madame, you bring me soup—purée of green peas. This is soup indeed. What flavour! What genial warmth! Madame, it goes to my heart. Never have I tasted anything so appetising, so nourishing, so consoling. Believe me, it is not in Quebec that one eats such soup."

"Monsieur," said Madame Giroux, beaming upon the stranger. "I am pleased to know that you like the soup. Now try a little of the ragout, if you please. You will find it tasty, I hope."

"Madame, you will not need to ask me twice, I assure you. Such a ragout after such a soup! I have no words. I am silenced. I can only ask for more of that ragout, and then a little more. Madame Giroux, this is the place I have been dreaming about all the year, all through the long winter, and now for two days I escape from the heat and dust of the city, and here I am—in Paradise. Here I would stay for the rest of my life. Ah, how I love the peace, the solitude of this place, where one has such an appetite and where one is regaled with such delicacies! Some more ragout? Ah, no, Madame, it is enough. Never do I eat to the point of surfeit. Wild strawberries and cream, you say? Yes, I accept willingly. And a cup of hot tea? Certainly. And after that my pipe, with your permission. Truly, I am content. It is a good world, is it not ? "

" But yes, Monsieur, it is the world of the good God."

" Ah ! I had not thought of that. On the contrary, I have often thought it the world of the devil. Back there in the city it is surely so, but in these mountains it may be that the good God still resides. Who can tell ? At least, there are good people here. That son of yours, Madame—he is a brave lad, and quite intelligent. He is no stupid habitant, not he. Quite different from the others—one sees that. He has studied, even, has he not, Madame ? "

" But yes, Monsieur, he has studied, very much. We were going to make a priest of him, but he would not. It was a pity, was it not ? "

" A pity ? Yes, a pity that you ever thought of it. To make a priest of Hector ! To put a *soutane* on Achilles ! To make him sit in a little box while young ladies come to confess their sins, their most grievous sins ! Ha ! Ha ! No, that is not for him. For others, perhaps, but for him work and war and love. That is his vocation. But there he comes. Look at him. Have you ever seen a more perfect model of a man ; a true Greek of the heroic age ? "

" Well, my friend, you are coming to supper at last, and you have an appetite like a wolf. I also had an appetite, but it is gone, because of a certain soup of green peas and a certain ragout, besides other dainties. But do not fear, I have left something for you. Fall to, my brave one. Enjoy the good things of life. Meanwhile I will show you my tackle, the apparatus with which I shall catch your trout. Look, my brave habitant, have you ever seen a collection like this ? "

The City Man thereupon unrolled his kit, and displayed before the astonished eyes of Madame Giroux and Jean the most complete assemblage of fishing tackle ever seen in St. Placide. There were lancewood rods of the finest stock, with delicate tips so slender that one would think they could not hold a minnow, and yet so tough that, in the hands of a skilful angler, they might draw in a salmon, though not without a long struggle. There were reels of gunmetal and oxidized silver, thin lines of the finest silk, casting-lines of gut and horse-hair, and a book of choice flies of every kind, from the modest March Brown and the plain Grey Hackle to the handsome Silver Doctor and the gaudy Jock Scott.

"*Mon Dieu*, Monsieur," said Jean, "you have all that is necessary, certainly. There is not a trout in the St. Ange that will be able to resist you."

"That is what I think," said the City Man, with a confident smile. "We shall catch fish to-morrow, you may be sure. And here is a little steelyard for weighing the big ones. It goes up to five pounds. We shall not take a trout bigger than that in this stream."

"I think not," said Jean. "It is very seldom that so large a fish is caught. If we get one of two pounds we shall do well. In former times there were plenty of big trout, and there are some left, but it is not easy to catch them. It demands skill and patience."

"If that is all," said the City Man, "we shall get them. You will see, my brave Jean. Look, for example, at this little book, a record of my achievements for the past four years. See! Stoneham, June 17th, 1895, 54 trout; June 18th, 55; June 19th, 68, of which the smallest was 8 inches in length and the largest, 16 inches. Again, Metabetchouan, Lac St. Jean, June 10th, 1896, 33 ouananiche, running from 1 to 5 pounds. Once more, Restigouche, July 5th, 1897, two salmon of 15 pounds each, one of 19 pounds, and one of 25 pounds. I could go on, but that is enough to show you that I have caught fish in my day, thousands of trout, hundreds of salmon, besides black bass innumerable, pike, too, and maskinongé, that tiger of the Canadian rivers. Yes, I claim to be an angler, a faithful disciple of the good Sir Isaac.

"You smile, my rural friend? Well, to-morrow I will show you. You will take your bamboo pole, your clothes line and your fat worms, while I will take one of my light rods, a thin silk line, a delicate cast, and those flies, as many as may be necessary, and at the end of the day we shall see. Yes, we shall see, my little demigod, my Ajax of the parish. If I do not take two trout for every one of yours, and the biggest fish of the day, I will give you my best rod and my book of flies, and I will eat my boots by way of penance. What do you say? Shall we have a contest for the championship of the St. Ange?"

"Willingly," said Jean, "but with your permission I will not use the bamboo pole of which you speak, nor the fat worms. I also have a liking for fly-fishing, and I should like to enter the contest on equal terms. If you win, Monsieur, which is more than likely, I shall be glad to have you take as the spoils of war the arms of the vanquished. But as for eating boots, you will excuse me, Monsieur, if I have no appetite for that."

"*Mon Dieu*, Monsieur Jean de St. Placide de St. Ange, but you have the true spirit of the olden time. And he fishes with a fly; the little habitant of the mountains uses the weapons of chivalry. Good! We shall have a tourney for trout, for glory, for the love of ladies. And I will overthrow you, so to speak, carry away your sword, your spear, your coat of mail, and put your name in my little book. Ha! ha! It will be sport indeed, and war—yes, war to the death.

"But meanwhile, my good Jean, we are the best of friends, are we not? You do not mind my innocent persiflage, I am sure. It is but the effervescence of spirits too long confined in the narrow conventions of city life, a little bubbling over of froth on the top of good liquor. Were it not for that I should burst, I think, at the heart. Ah, the blessed country! What relief, what freedom, what recreation! But it occurs to me that a good sleep would be the best preparation for the struggle of the coming day. Is it not so, Jean? Madame, with your permission I will take my candle. Madame, I retire. I bid you good-night. Until four o'clock, Jean, my dear enemy."

At four o'clock Jean aroused the City Man from a dreamless sleep; at half-past four they had breakfast; and an hour later they were setting up their rods by the St. Ange, at a place where the river was broad and a strong man could ford the stream.

"This is where I usually begin," said Jean, "for it is a good place to cross. If you will take the other side you will find good fishing."

"No doubt," said the City Man, "the fishing must be good over there since few men could cross that current. But I will take no advantage, my friend. You shall cross and I will fish on this side."

"But no, Monsieur, you do not know the stream, as I do. Pass over, if you please."

" Not at all, Jean, I will not. But wait. Let us toss a coin. Heads, you go across, tails, I go."

" Tails," said Jean.

" It is tails, Jean, so you have your way, after all. Well, here goes, my brave one. I will take the other side according to the hazard, and meet you somewhere above, later in the day. *Au revoir*, Jean."

" *Au revoir*, Monsieur, and good luck to you."

The City Man waded into the stream, and when he reached the middle, standing in three feet of swift water, he made a dexterous cast and immediately hooked a fine, half-pound trout. After a brief struggle he brought the fish to hand, and held it up with a shout of triumph.

" There, Jean," he called, above the noise of the water. " First blood! Begin, my brave one, you have no time to lose. Begin, begin."

Thus the contest began, and all day the rivals fished up the stream, trying their best to outdo each other both in numbers and size. The day was perfect, with alternating sun and shade, and a light breeze that raised a ripple on the pools, and in both pools and rapids the hungry trout rose eagerly to the fly. Jean passed quickly along, contenting himself with taking one or two fish in every good place, while the City Man patiently whipped every foot of the stream. In some pools he took four or five trout, and there was not a likely place where he did not catch at least one fish.

Soon Jean was far ahead, but the City Man paid no attention to him. Enjoying the solitude, the sound of the water, the voice of the breeze, the delicious mountain air, he took keen delight in examining with a practised eye every pool and riffle, every possible lurking-place for the agile, wary trout. In this swift water he would take an eight-inch fish, behind that rock in midstream he would hook a ten-inch trout that would fight like a veteran; in that deep pool beneath the shade of an overhanging pine he might hope to take a trout weighing at least a pound, with a chance of capturing a big fish, the prize of the day.

It was glorious sport, the best that the City Man had ever known, and it had for him an added zest in the thought of the contest with his rustic adversary, the triumph that would be his, and the trophy that he was going to win. It was not a very fine rod, that of Jean Baptiste, but it would be an interesting memento of his visit to St. Placide, and a further proof of his claim to the title of champion angler of the Province. So the City Man went on fishing all the day, never once relaxing his efforts, not even stopping to eat the good luncheon that Madame Giroux had provided. The morning passed; the afternoon wore away; while the City Man's pannier was gradually filled, until there was not room for another trout. Then he noticed that the sun was sinking, and the shadows creeping down the mountainside.

"*Mon Dieu*," he said to himself, "I had no idea that it was so late. And we must be at least four miles from the house. How heavy that pannier! A good catch, certainly. But where is my poor Jean Baptiste? I have not seen him since the early morning. Ah, there he is on the other side, sitting on a big rock and smoking his pipe as though at peace with himself and all the world. He has given up the contest, that is clear. Well, the poor devil must have some consolation. But I wonder how long he has been there."

"*Holà*, Jean! *Holà*, there! Can one cross at this place?"

"Yes, Monsieur," called Jean. "This is the best ford on the river. Come right over. The water is not at all deep."

"Well, my brave one," said the City Man, as he stepped out of the water. "Well, my noble angler, and did you catch some fish? Did they take worms to-day?"

"You forget, Monsieur, that we were to fish with flies."

"Oh, yes, very true. And you have done it? It was hard work, was it not? It demands skill, as you have discovered. But do not be discouraged. Cheer up. You will learn in the course of time. A young man of your intelligence can learn anything. Come now, how many did you take?"

"I have not counted them, Monsieur," said Jean, "but I see that you have made a good catch, a very good catch."

"A good catch? Well, I may say so," said the City Man, a little nettled. "It is the catch of my life. See! I will pour them out on the pebbles. Yes, a nice pile of trout. Let us count them. One—two—three . . . seventy-two — seventy-three — seventy-four — all good fish—and this two-pounder makes seventy-five. A good day's work. Yes, Jean, there are trout in this river, but it takes skill to catch them. It is all in a little turn of the wrist. I will teach you. But show your fish. If you have thirty-eight trout, I lose."

"Well," said Jean, with a smile, getting his pannier from the cool shade of the rock, "I think that I have at least thirty-eight. Let us see. One — two — three —four . . . thirty-seven — thirty-eight — thirty-nine

... seventy-four — seventy-five — seventy-six ... eighty-eight — eighty-nine — ninety. There, Monsieur, that is not bad—ninety good trout; and this one, the brother of yours; and this other, the grandfather of both. There, that is all."

The City Man was speechless. He gasped in astonishment, grew pale for a moment, then red in the face; but presently, as he gazed on the wonderful catch, his equanimity returned, and with it a glow of enthusiasm for the angler who had shown a prowess so unexpected, so utterly admirable. Turning to Jean with an air of new and profound respect, he said:

"Monsieur Giroux, I salute you as the most perfect angler of the Province. More than that, I say, I, Gaspard Trudel, that there is not your equal in the whole of Canada. Accept, I beg of you, this rod of mine. It was a trophy, and I have used it with pride, but now it will be in more worthy hands. Monsieur Giroux, once more I salute you."

Two days later, as Jean was driving Monsieur Trudel back to the city, they talked much of the future industrial development of St. Placide. Monsieur Trudel was a man of vision, and entered with enthusiasm into Jean's plans and ambitions, declaring that an angler of such eminence could attain the same distinction in other fields of effort and would succeed in anything that he might undertake. But the sportsman was also an astute lawyer and man of affairs, and wisely counselled Jean to make haste slowly, step by step, overcoming minor obstacles as they were encountered and gaining strength and experience by which he should remove mountains in the course of time. Meanwhile, there was the farm to manage, the mail contract to fulfil, and if bed and board could be provided for sportsmen such as he, it would be easy to find many tired men from the city who would gladly spend their holidays in such a paradise. So it was Monsieur Trudel who, for good or ill, first suggested to Jean the exploitation of the summer tourist.

CHAPTER IX

THE LOAN

"IF I am not mistaken," said Monsieur Trembly, the notary, with a shrewd smile, "it is, in effect, a hotel that you would be building at St. Placide, a house of twelve rooms, by far the largest in the parish. Your good friend Monsieur Trudel has told me all about it. A great sportsman, he. A good advocate, of course, a Q.C., in line for the bench, and all that, but a sportsman above all, and an angler, the most skilful in the Province. He has discovered St. Placide, it seems, and would like you to build a hotel for himself and his brother anglers. Not a bad idea. But it will cost money to build a place like that—as much as five thousand dollars, perhaps."

"No, Monsieur Trembly," said Jean, with assurance, "not half of that sum. The logs I will cut myself, during the winter; in the spring the neighbours will help me to raise the frame; for a couple of months we shall need carpenters, and then, before the end of June, at the beginning of the tourist season, the house will be completed at a cost of less than two thousand dollars, including furniture. Certainly, two thousand dollars will be more than sufficient."

"Well," said the notary, "we can obtain the money, I think. A certain client of mine will let us have it. If not, Monsieur Trudel will advance the amount, or

I will do so myself, if necessary. The enterprise is most promising, certainly, and you have other plans, I am told. You will build a dam, a mill, a factory, in the course of time. It may be that you are running some risk, but if all goes well you will be a rich man, and at the same time a benefactor to the whole parish. That is what I call true success, Monsieur Giroux."

"And the security will be ample. It is your mother's farm that you would hypothecate, a good property, indeed, one hundred acres of arable land, a hundred of pasture, two hundred of forest—a fief of the Seminary, subject to the usual dues, which are a mere bagatelle. It is a fine property, not very saleable, perhaps, in these times, but should fetch five thousand dollars, possibly six, at a forced sale. Yes, certainly, you shall have the money—two thousand dollars for three years, interest at eight per cent., payable half-yearly. I will have the papers drawn at once. Come again in a few days, Monsieur Giroux, and all will be arranged."

Jean was not altogether happy about mortgaging his mother's farm, but the projects which he had in mind could be realized in no other way. Since the visit of the City Man there had been a constant stream of visitors, chiefly fishermen; and when, at the close of the season, he cast up his accounts, he discovered a profit of a hundred dollars from this source alone, besides the allowance from the Government and the enhanced revenue from farm produce sold in the Quebec markets. It was a veritable mine of wealth that he had discovered, and a vista of unlimited possibilities opened before him.

At first there would be the new house of twelve rooms,

providing accommodation for twenty or thirty guests; but presently the building would be enlarged; cottages for whole families would be built; there would be grassy courts for tennis and croquet, horses for riding and driving, canoes for the river, guides for excursions to distant lakes and streams, and even provision for the winter, when stalwart hunters would come to chase moose and caribou. The valley of the St. Ange, too long neglected, with its beautiful mountains, grand forests, clear air, and pure water, its hunting and fishing, would become one of the most celebrated resorts in the Province, frequented by rich citizens of Quebec and Montreal, wealthy English tourists, and American millionaires. Jean himself, the originator of the movement, would be the first to share in the profits, but the influx of tourists would bring prosperity to the whole parish and lay the foundations for still greater things in the years to come.

But the neighbours, for whose benefit the great work was to be done, did not look upon it with kindly eyes. On the contrary, they were filled with envy, and their gossip about the doings of Jean Baptiste was far from charitable. That a young man should aspire to become a priest was in the order of nature, an ambition to be respected and encouraged. As such, he would be an honour to the family and a credit to the parish; but that he should attempt to set up a new industry, to forsake the traditions of the fathers, to walk in untrodden paths, was an innovation unheard of and most disquieting, a defiance of sacred custom, a rebellion, indeed, against religion and the Holy Church.

Moreover, the effects of such changes upon the morals of the people, especially the young, would be sad indeed. One had but to consider the ways of city people to see that they were frivolous in their behaviour, light in their conversation and worldly in their dress. Their influence was altogether bad, as could be seen in places like Malbaie and Cacouna, where the young maidens, even, once so industrious and pious, were filling their minds with the foolish notions of the city. No longer would they wear the modest costumes of their mothers and grandmothers, but were imitating the dress of high society, made, it was said, according to fashions devised by men tailors in the great and wicked city of Paris. Once the summer tourists established themselves in St. Placide, the simplicity and contentment of former days would be gone; religion and virtue would be no more; and the young people would enter the mad race for wealth, fashion, and all the follies and vanities of the world.

Besides, the tourist business was not profitable after all. More revenue was taken in, to be sure, but one's expenses increased in still greater degree, and in the end one stood face to face with ruin and bankruptcy. Such would be the fate of Jean Baptiste and of all who were carried away by his plausible schemes. No, he must not be allowed to ruin the people, to corrupt their morals, to endanger their immortal souls. Something should be done; some one should interfere, to put Jean Baptiste in his proper place or to drive him away from the parish.

The good neighbours did not at first see the matter in that light, but when it was brought to their notice by certain malicious spirits, they were not slow to recognize the danger of the proposed innovations and to condemn unheard one whom they did not understand. Even the best friends of Jean Baptiste were somewhat influenced by this talk, and their minds were poisoned by the insidious gossip.

Gabrielle, also, within the sacred precincts of the Ursuline Convent, heard rumours of the doings of Jean Baptiste. There was no other girl from St. Placide at the convent, but Adèle Couture of L'Ange Gardien was there, who now and then received letters from her cousin and bosom friend Mélanie Couture, containing not only fragments of gossip about Jean, but whole pages of news, telling of all his doings during the past summer, of the great house that he was going to build, and the innovations that he was about to introduce into the once peaceful and happy parish. So busy was he with his work in the woods, where he was preparing logs for his new house, that one scarcely caught a glimpse of him except on Wednesdays and Saturdays, when he carried the mail; but on those occasions he would always smile and bow and give a cheerful good-day to any of the neighbours whom he might see as he passed along. Certainly, he seemed to be in high spirits, well pleased with himself and all the world, as a young man of such gifts might well be, with all the world at his feet, not excepting the girls of the parish, not one of whom would say him nay. But it was impossible to discover that Jean showed preference for any, unless it were Blanchette Laroche, that old creature with the speckled face, twenty-six years of age at the very least, but of an amiable temper, of great capacity as a housekeeper, and with the expectation of an ample dowry. Not that Jean had ever paid her any special attention, beyond what might be expected of a good neighbour, but there were signs that showed how the wind blew, and developments might be expected at any time.

All this and more Adèle read to her friend Gabrielle, and together they talked and laughed about the backwoods hero as young girls do who are fancy free and who take pleasure in idealizing a common man by making of him a hero in disguise, riding forth to do battle for the two-fold prize of glory and his lady's love. But, strange to say, Gabrielle did not tell her friend that Jean was other than a former schoolfellow and casual acquaintance; nor did she give the watchful Adèle the slightest cause to suspect that her "habitant," "mail-driver," and "inn-keeper" was more often in her thoughts than a certain brave officer of artillery, or a certain young teller in the Banque Nationale.

But the rumours that came to Gabrielle were disquieting, and interfered with her studies in art and literature more than she would have dared to confess, even to herself. She was happy in the convent, in the companionship of her fellow-pupils and under the direction of the sweet-faced sisters; she loved the Mother Superior and applied herself with devotion to her religious duties; but her thoughts often wandered to St. Placide, where one who had loved her long was proving by manly deeds his right to claim that she should love him in return.

She did not love him, no, not yet; but it was pleasant to think of that young man, her hero and knight, girding on his armour, taking a noble part in the battle of life, overcoming all obstacles, casting down all enemies, making a place in the world and an honourable name—and all for her. Poor Jean! He had been faithful for a long time and deserved some little encouragement, some slight reward. Gabrielle blushed as she thought of that, and wished that she had not been so cruel to Jean when last they met. It would be necessary to atone, but when and how?

Gabrielle was sure of Jean's devotion, and yet there were times when she thought him altogether too gay and debonair in the absence of his lady-love, too free with his smiles, too ready to greet the young women of the parish as he drove by, too confident altogether, considering the slight encouragement that he had received. It almost seemed as though he had never loved her with his whole heart, else why was he not more cast down and why so easily consoled? But to whom could he go for consolation? Surely not to Blanchette Laroche. That would be too absurd. Doubtless, it was in his work that Jean found consolation, because it brought him nearer to his heart's desire. But Blanchette was clever and capable, a perfect housekeeper, a charming companion—if one could forget her face. Yet there was a strange sweetness about that face. Yes, it might be well to return to St. Placide for the Christmas vacation, just to be at home again for a little while, to get a glimpse of the old friends, and to have a little change from the monotony of convent life.

It was a glorious winter morning, on the Sunday after Gabrielle's return; and although she might have driven to church in the family berline, she preferred to walk, and started early, that she might fully enjoy the beauty of the winter landscape, breathe the clear, cold mountain air, and feel the life blood tingling in all her veins. As she came near the cottage of Mère Tabeau she quickened her pace, thinking to escape notice, but the old crone, like a spider, was lying in wait, and came forth just as Gabrielle, with face averted, was passing by.

"Wait a minute, Gabrielle—Mademoiselle Taché," she called. "Can you not wait, my dear? I, too, am going to Mass, although you may think it strange. Yes, I go to Mass every Sunday, and to confession too, when necessary. There are often little sins, you know. But how fast you walk, Gabrielle—Mademoiselle! A little slower, if you please. I like the company of the young and beautiful. They do not like my company, perhaps, those proud ones, those rich ones with the fine moccasins and the expensive furs, because they forget, the gay creatures, that one day they too may be old and poor and lame. Yes, and they don't know that misfortune may come to them at any time, and very soon—yes, indeed."

"*Mon Dieu*, Madame Tabeau!" said Gabrielle, a little frightened, "I did not intend to walk so fast. It is the frosty air, Madame, that makes the feet move. But I shall be glad to walk more slowly, for the pleasure of your company."

"The pleasure of my company! Ha! Ha! *Sacrée petite vierge!* That was well said. A lie, of course, but pleasing to hear, for all that. You have learned manners, it would seem, at the convent. The Ursuline ladies are nothing if not polite. I knew one of them myself, long ago, who could stab you to the heart and smile sweetly all the time. And she lives still, the assassin! Ah, serpent! What a pleasure it would be to crush thee in the dust!"

"But, Madame——"

"Yes, my dear. Yes, Mademoiselle Gabrielle. I forgot that you were there. Strange words for the ears of innocence. Strange tales for a Sunday morning on the way to Mass. Yes, let us change the subject. Let us talk of something more interesting—of Jean Baptiste Giroux, for example."

At this shaft Gabrielle flushed a little, almost imperceptibly, but said, with an assumption of indifference:

"Why of him, Madame Tabeau? I am not at all interested."

"She is not interested, the young lady, not at all. Why then does she blush, and why does her voice tremble at the mention of his name? Not interested, Mademoiselle Innocent? Then you do not dislike him, of course?"

"No, Madame Tabeau. It is a fine morning, is it not? How beautiful the snow and the blue shadows of the trees!"

"Yes, yes, of course. But why, I wonder, does Jean Baptiste spend every day in the woods, cutting down trees, making logs of every size, shaping them for the frame of a great house, hauling them to a certain place? Why all this preparation, Gabrielle, my dear?"

"How should I know, Madame Tabeau? He does not tell me of his plans."

"No? Not even that he borrowed two thousand dollars for the hotel that he is to build as soon as the snow is gone? He did not borrow it, then, from Monsieur your father?"

"Certainly not, Madame, I do not wish to discuss the question. What Monsieur Giroux does is nothing to me."

"Nothing to you? Of course not. Then he did not get the money from Monsieur Taché. And there are but two rich men in the parish. Ah, now we have it. From Monsieur Laroche, of course. That is what I thought at the first. Now all is clear, clear as day. A young man of marriageable age wishes to advance himself in the world; the daughter of a rich habitant is not unwilling; the good, wise young man proposes an alliance; secures the money and a housekeeper at the same time; kills two birds with one stone. Ha! Ha! The good, wise young man of marriageable age!

"He is a deep thinker, Jean Baptiste, a young man of prudence, foresight, strategy—all that. Yes, for such a house one must have a housekeeper, a cook and a maid of all work. See! He secures them all at one stroke. A stroke of genius, that. No matter that she is no beauty, that her face has been spoiled by the small-pox. She is capable, good-tempered, affectionate, and has an ample dowry—the best in the parish. What more could one desire? That explains those visits to the house of Bonhomme Laroche. Yes, it explains everything. The wedding will be in June, no doubt, before the beginning of the tourist season. It will be a great affair, with a feast and a grand dance. You will dance at the wedding, Mademoiselle Taché, will you not?"

Gabrielle's face was as white as the snow.

"Madame Tabeau," she said, scarcely maintaining her composure, "I have to say to you that these are vile lies which you are telling about Jean Baptiste. He may be foolish, as they say, but he is incapable of such baseness. Madame, this conversation is distasteful to me. Pass on, if you please, or stay behind. I wish to be alone."

The vicious old woman, abashed before the loyal

courage of Gabrielle, turned aside, muttering maledictions, and went to visit one of her cronies in the village, to learn the most recent gossip, and to tell of the significant discoveries she had made on the way to Church.

As for Gabrielle, she entered the Church alone, and as she knelt before the image of the Mother of God her body was shaken with sobs, and she could scarcely whisper the prayers that for two thousand years have brought consolation and courage to so many souls. But as the young girl prayed the peace of God descended into her soul; and when the congregation assembled and the service began, her voice, calm and clear, arose with theirs in humble confession, wistful supplication and joyous praise.

When the sacrifice of the Mass was over and the congregation had dispersed, Gabrielle remained kneeling for a long time, striving to forget the world, to fix her attention upon the Cross, to think only of her divine Redeemer. But this she could not do, for the thought of Jean filled her mind and heart; and she felt, with mingled pride and shame, that she loved him more than aught else in the world, and that the Kingdom of Heaven was as nothing to her compared with the kingdom of earthly love.

And Jean loved her in return. Had he not told her so? Yes, but she had sent him away in anger, and now it was another that he loved. Impossible! No, for who could tell what love might do? Yet his first love she would always have. Always! And this also was possible, in all the chance and caprice of love, that he might come back to her, penitent, asking forgiveness. It would not be hard to forgive Jean, if only he would come ; but what if it were too late, and the day of love were gone forever ?

Ah, that lovely morning so long ago, when she did not love, or loved all the world, and no one had taken her love away ! The pity, the cruelty of it ! The moment love was found enshrined in the heart, that moment it was snatched away. The bright vision appeared, was gone, and would not return. Oh, it could not be, must not be, not even if it were the will of God. No, she could not give him up, would not. She would fight for him against all the world—to the death. Ah, Lord Jesus ! It was He who had gone to the death for the world, for her. What sin, what mortal sin to love mortal man more than the Redeemer of the world ! And the sacrifice—was it not the law of life and death, of time and eternity ?

Gabrielle was rebellious no more, but bowed her head in humiliation and sorrow, with chastened spirit and sincere repentance repeating the morning prayer :

" Holy Virgin, Mother of God, my mother and my friend, I place myself under your protection and implore your pity. Be, O Mother of Kindness, my refuge in my need, my consolation in my troubles, and my advocate with your dear Son, all the days of my life, and especially in the hour of death.

" Angel of Heaven, my faithful and charitable guide, obtain for me the grace to be so docile and teachable that my footsteps may never stray from the way of the commandments of my God.

" Yes, my God, I love you with all my heart, with all my soul, with all my spirit, with all my power, and I promise to love my neighbour as myself for the love of you."

When Gabrielle left the Church and came out again

into the clear light of day, the agony and struggle of the past hour seemed like an evil dream. The snow was as white and pure as ever, the sky as blue, and the bright sunlight streamed all about like a radiance from God. She took long breaths of the delicious, frosty air that went tingling through her veins like wine, and along the crisp surface of road she went tripping on light moccasined feet, while her eyes shone and her face glowed with the joy of living. What could it be that had troubled her so? Who was that old witch with the evil eye that had put such thoughts into her head? Jean was hers, without a doubt. He was not one to change or be discouraged because of a girl's saucy words. When he was ready he would ask, and take no refusal. But if not, what matter? There were others—a certain young officer of the Garrison, for example. Jean was not indispensable, by any means. Blanchette might have him at any time. No, not Blanchette, but any other girl in the parish—Suzette Gagnon, for example, with her coal-black hair, her pale complexion, her green eyes, and no dowry at all. Yes, Suzette it should be, for punishment.

As Gabrielle was disposing of her lover in this summary way, she became aware of footsteps behind her, and in a moment a tall, stalwart form was walking by her side, and she knew, without looking, that it was Jean himself, aggressive as ever and very much the master of his own destiny.

"Good morning, Gabrielle," he said, as if they had always been the best of friends. "Is it permitted that one walk along with you for a distance?"

"The road is free, Monsieur Giroux, and you have overtaken me. You walk too fast."

"Oh, no, Gabrielle, but I am glad that you walk so slowly. Of what were you thinking, I wonder?"

Gabrielle blushed at the too pointed question, but laughed at her own confusion.

"There is an inquisitive man, I must say; and a conceited man too. Perhaps he believes that I was thinking of him."

"Ah! if you only were, Gabrielle! For me, I certainly was thinking of you. I saw you in Church, and heard you too. *Mon Dieu*, but you sing like an angel."

"Monsieur Giroux," said Gabrielle, reprovingly, "you should go to Church to pray, to worship, and not to look at the neighbours."

"The neighbours, Gabrielle — were they there? I saw but one. And I worship, I pray—this is what I pray: 'God give me the beautiful angel whom I adore!'"

"Jean!" said Gabrielle, with a radiant smile, "you must not talk like that—it is wicked. But tell me what is it that you do in the woods every day. Why all this industry, I wonder? Why is the mighty hunter not on the hills chasing the moose, the caribou, the bear?"

"Gabrielle, the bear sleeps all winter, and I have been asleep for many years. Now, I am awaking, and I begin to see the opportunities of life. I see and seize them as they come along. First I become habitant, then mail driver, then I build a house for tourists, and after that—well, after that we shall see. Gabrielle, it is not true that I am a good-for-nothing. Say that it is not true."

"Jean, my friend, forgive me. I did not mean it, as you know. You are a hero, my hero, since the day when you saved me from the river. You remember, do you not? But walk on the other side of the road, if you please. I have only one question to ask, one little question. Jean Baptiste, why did you borrow the money from Bonhomme Laroche? Answer me—quick, quick! Oh, *Mon Dieu! Mon Dieu!* he did it!"

"But, Gabrielle, I do not understand."

"Monsieur Giroux," said Gabrielle, her eyes flaming with indignation, "do not lie to me. You understand very well. Please to step out of the way."

"Gabrielle, my dear Gabrielle, it was a mistake, a blunder. I can explain."

"Will Monsieur Giroux step out of the way, or shall I call my father?"

"*Sacré!*" said Jean, in a burst of anger, turning his back on Gabrielle, and striding rapidly down the hill, exploding imprecations as he went. "*Sacré tonnerre!* Fool of a woman! Little fool! But what a dear little fool! What perversity, what unreason! But what dear perversity, what charming unreason! Angel of Heaven! Give her up? Ah, not yet, not for that. I will win her—I swear it. This also I will accomplish with the help of God and Saint Jean Baptiste."

CHAPTER X

BLANCHETTE

"*Bonjour*, Jean Baptiste," said Bonhomme Laroche, one spring morning, approaching the place where Jean was working on the frame of his new house, now almost ready for the raising. "The work moves along, I see."

"*Bonjour*, Monsieur Laroche," said Jean, as pleasantly as possible, wishing to be polite to the old man. "Yes, the work is well along. Next week we shall have the raising, and in ten weeks more all will be finished."

"Very good, Jean, very good indeed. And how is the money holding out? Two thousand dollars is not a great sum for a work of such magnitude."

"I have not touched it Monsieur Laroche. That is for the carpenters, for furniture, for horses, carts, and the like. Never fear, Monsieur. It will be more than sufficient."

"You have not touched it yet? What economy! And you pay interest all the time, merely to make sure of the loan. What prudence, what foresight! Well, money is not so easy to get in St. Placide, where all the people are poor, but in Quebec there are rich men, bankers, capitalists. Ha! Ha! So one gets a loan of two thousand dollars in Quebec, and one pays interest to a poor habitant of St. Placide—as an act of charity, merely. *Mon Dieu*, it is to laugh."

"Monsieur Laroche," said Jean, with some asperity,

"it was a trick that you played on me, and I do not appreciate the humour of it. I had no idea that Monsieur Trembly was an agent of yours. But you have your security, and as to the money, I do not intend to give it back to you at present."

"Do not think of it, my friend. The money is yours for the time, so long as you pay the interest when due—eight per cent., payable half-yearly. And do not be grateful, either. It was not for gratitude that I made the loan, but for a first mortgage on one of the best farms in the parish. I should like well to add that farm to mine. What a fine block I should have—an estate of some magnitude! Be careful to pay the interest on the day, my friend.

"But do not let us quarrel, Jean. Perhaps you may be my son-in-law some day—who knows? Stranger things have happened in this strange world. And I do not hesitate to tell you that it would please me well. As to Blanchette, she would make no objection. It is a dutiful child, that. I say to her: 'Marry Jean Baptiste, my daughter,' and she replies: 'I cannot disobey you, my dear father, although I have no special fancy for the young man.' Jean, my lad, would it not be a good arrangement?"

"Monsieur Laroche," said Jean, earnestly, "you are pleased to be facetious, but I have to tell you that I do not like your proposals, which would be as distasteful to Mademoiselle Blanchette as to myself. I am not thinking of marriage for the present, but when I do it will not be for land, nor houses, nor the loan of two thousand dollars. Your interest, Monsieur Laroche you shall have upon the day; and when the principal is due I will pay you with the greatest pleasure."

"Oh, my dear Jean, not so fiery, if you please. No offence was intended—only the proposal of an honourable alliance, honourable and advantageous. The Laroches are of a good family, my friend, respectable cultivators for ten generations. Blanchette will not take offence, I am sure, and why should you? No, Jean, let us be good neighbours, as always. As to the interest, do not be too particular. What is that between friends? You may even need the accommodation of a further loan. That also we can arrange. We are old neighbours, you know. I had a high regard for your good father, and I have always looked upon you as a promising young man, a youth who will go far, with the backing of friends and money. Such things are not to be despised."

"Monsieur Laroche," said Jean, somewhat ashamed of his hasty words, "you mean well, I am sure, and I thank you. Forgive my impatience. I dare say that I did not understand."

"Say no more, Jean. We understand each other pretty well, after all. You are a young man of ideas, and I also have some ideas, strange to say. We might exchange views, might we not, to our mutual advantage? We must have a talk, many talks. Come to see me, Jean, this very evening. We shall have a good dinner and a good talk. Blanchette will be there, of course, but do not fear—she will not bite you."

Jean could not well refuse the proffered courtesy of the old fox, and thus it came about that he paid his second visit to the Maison Laroche, and at dinner found himself seated at the hospitable board with the old man and Blanchette, surprisingly contented and hugely entertained by the conversation of the shrewd old miser and his clever daughter.

"And so, Monsieur Jean Baptiste Giroux," said Blanchette, with a smile of amusement, " you are the young man whom my father wishes me to marry, are you not ? "

" Mademoiselle," stammered Jean, taken aback, " Monsieur your father is very kind, I am sure."

" Not at all, Jean my lad," broke in Bonhomme Laroche, rubbing his hands in delight. " It is what I have always wished. A young man of your talents is not so easy to find in these days. In my day it was different. Then there were tall, handsome youths in plenty, and beautiful girls as well. Your mother, Blanchette, was the most beautiful of all. Ah, those were days ! But now, my friend, it seems to me that you are the only youth in the parish who compares with those of former times. Is it not so, Blanchette ? "

" It may well be, my father, although I have no memory of that time. Truly, Monsieur Giroux, I am still quite young—on the sunny side of thirty, I assure you. Your mother will tell you that I have the advantage of you by only a year and a day. But without flattery I will say that you compare very well with the other young men of the parish, even those who have gone away. Pamphile was tall and strong, but he had not your intelligence. Monsieur Giroux, Jean, I have a mind to accept you."

" You do me too much honour, Mademoiselle," murmured Jean, much embarrassed, and wondering how he was going to escape from a situation so difficult.

" Not so fast, Jean, not so fast. Look before you leap, my friend. I am not beautiful, as you see."

"Mademoiselle," said Jean, insincerely, "it is the beauty of the spirit that counts."

"You do not mean that, Jean, and yet I like to hear you say it. Moreover, it is more true than you think. I have read; I have travelled; I have thought much upon the vanities of the world. Oh, yes, I have cultivated the graces of the spirit to make up for my lack in other respects. And I was beautiful once, before the smallpox. Can you believe it?"

"She is beautiful still, Jean," broke in the old man. "For me, I find her just the same, the very image of her mother."

"Ah, my good father, if all the young men were like you I should not die an old maid."

"You shall not, Blanchette, you shall not. Notice, Jean Baptiste, only notice what a fine housekeeper she is. Look at the table, the chairs, the windows, the curtains, the stove, even, how proper they are; and the floor—one could eat off it. And what a cook! Confess, Jean, that you have never tasted roast chicken better than that which you are now eating."

"It is true, Monsieur," said Jean, with enthusiasm. "The chicken is perfect, of a tenderness unequalled, of a flavour incomparable."

"But wait," continued the old man, with an air of mystery. "There is better still to come. Blanchette, the dessert. We will surprise our guest. Madame Giroux is a famous cook, but not in the same class with you, my dear."

"There, my father, you have said enough," laughed Blanchette, stopping his mouth with her open palm. "Be still, now, or you will frighten Monsieur Giroux, and he will never come again. Never mind him, Jean;

he is only a foolish old man who is blinded by love. You could not be thus blinded, could you, my friend?"

"But the dessert, Blanchette, the dessert. I will say no more if only you will bring it in, instantly."

"Ah, I had forgotten," said Blanchette, going to the cupboard and bringing thence an immense plate of *croquignoles* of all sizes and shapes, delicately powdered with white sugar.

"There, Messieurs; there is the *tour de force*. If you have not eaten too much chicken, perhaps you will enjoy the *croquignoles*. And I have a little bottle of currant wine, too, to finish. Monsieur Giroux, I drink to our better acquaintance."

"And I," said Jean, quite disarmed by the kindness of those whom he had thought to be his enemies, "to your health, Mademoiselle Blanchette! To yours, Monsieur Laroche! Permit me to say that I have never tasted currant wine so delicious, and that the *croquignoles* are beyond all praise."

"They are not so bad, Jean, and I am glad that you like them. As you see, my friend, I have made a study of human nature, and I know how to please men by good food and drink—and a little flattery."

"Well, Mademoiselle, you succeed marvellously, I must confess."

"Yes, Jean; but, as you may have observed, I have this time omitted the flattery."

"Mademoiselle, it is lucky for me that you have omitted something, else I should have surrendered without the honours of war."

"That would not do at all, Jean. He who gives to me his hand gives his heart also, and must be able to say, with a certain king: 'All is lost save honour.' Could you say that?"

"Mademoiselle, what shall I say? You are a sorceress, I think."

"But no, Jean, only one who observes. It is like walking through the forest where there are signs that one may read if one has eyes to see. And there are little birds, too, that tell one things. But tell me; how does your house advance? It will soon be finished, will it not?"

"Very soon, Mademoiselle—in ten weeks, or less."

"Good. I am delighted to hear it. See, I will give you a toast, neighbour Jean. To your health, to the health of all whom you love. To your success in everything—everything. Do you understand?"

"Yes, Blanchette, I understand, and I thank you."

"What are you saying, you two?" said the old man. "Why all this mysterious talk? For me, I do not understand at all. Yet you have your secrets, I suppose."

"Naturally," said Blanchette, smiling. "We have at least one great secret. Shall I tell him, Jean? Shall I tell you, my father? As to this Jean Baptiste, I like him very much, and we are going to be the best of friends, but I will not marry him. Say nothing—I will not."

The old man stared at his daughter for some moments in mingled anger and amazement; but presently, his reason getting the better of his rage, he replied, in the tone of an indulgent parent to a wayward child:

"There, Blanchette, my dear, no one is asking you to marry anybody. What have I done? I have merely asked the young man to dine with us, to eat of our roast chicken and *croquignoles*, to see what a fine housekeeper you are, to perceive how happy one can be in a home of one's own—that is all. Do not trouble yourself. You shall marry or not, just as you please. Yes, you shall stay with your old father, little one, until the very end. But after that it will be lonely for you, will it not ? "

" My good father," said Blanchette, gently caressing his grizzled hair, " do not talk like that. You are still a young man, as any one can see, and I shall be with you for many years. Let us not consider a future so remote. But in the worst case there is always the convent for old maids like me."

" The convent ? Holy Virgin ! What would you do in a convent, Blanchette, with your beauty, your accomplishments ? Cut off your long hair, hide your lovely face behind a black veil, pray at midnight on the cold stones ? No, no, Mignonne. Leave that to the old, the ugly, the disappointed. For you the fireside, a loving husband, beautiful children, the management of the house—all that makes life worth while. Besides, you are not pious enough for the religious life. You have no vocation. No, it is not for you."

" My father," said Blanchette, " have you finished at last ? Monsieur Giroux wishes to go, I think. *Au revoir*, Monsieur Jean. It has been a great pleasure to have seen you. Come again soon. Good neighbours should meet often, should they not ? "

" Yes, Jean," assented the old man, " Come often— every day if you like. I shall be glad to see you. As for Blanchette, never mind what she says. Women are changeable, as you know. But if not, if not, Jean

Baptiste Giroux, take care; keep out of my way; for I will crush you like a snake."

Jean laughed. "Do not trouble yourself, Monsieur Laroche; I shall be safe enough, never fear. But I thank you for your hospitality; and you, Mademoiselle Blanchette, for all that and for your good wishes as well."

As Jean took the road toward his own home the night was dark, with lowering clouds on the hills, and a chill April wind blew from patches of unmelted snow. He was stumbling along, uncertain of the way, when a beam of light shone out from a lamp set in the window of the Maison Laroche.

"It is Blanchette," said Jean to himself, "and the light which she throws on the path will guide me for some distance yet. One can take a good many steps on a dark night, if one sees a friendly gleam in a window here and there."

CHAPTER XI

LA FOLIE

" Is it possible ? " said Father Paradis to Jean Baptiste on a fine afternoon in June. " Can it be that your great house is finished and ready for the tourists so early in the season ? It is incredible, marvellous, but there it stands, and one must believe one's own eyes, I suppose. Truly, Jean, my son, you have accomplished a great work."

" Yes, Monsieur," said Jean, with a glow of pride. " It is finished at last, thank God, and I am well content. But will you not come in to see the place, Monsieur le curé ? "

" Yes, indeed," said the curé, " I must see it all, from cellar to attic, for you are as a son to me and I am interested in everything that you do. Let us begin with the cellar, the foundation of things."

" This way, Monsieur le curé. It is not far underground, as you see, and the windows are large, for the sake of light and air. But it is always cool in summer and sufficiently warm in winter, and dry as well. Here is our dairy. There is the cream separator, of which we are very proud, and there is the churn, of an improved pattern. It is not much work, in these days, to take care of the milk of a dozen cows."

" But where, Jean, are the potatoes, turnips, onions, and all that ? In my day we used to keep them in the cellar ; and the ham, the bacon, the sausages, the dried apples and the tobacco we used to hang to the beams of the kitchen, where they were well smoked and dried, you may be sure. Yes, and well covered with dust and flies. But now all that is changed, no doubt. This scientific housekeeping is truly wonderful."

"Yes," said Jean, with a smile, "we have now different arrangements. Vegetables are excellent, in their place, but they do not improve the flavour of the butter; so we keep them in another part of the cellar, well isolated, as you will see."

Father Paradis was greatly interested in exploring every part of the cellar, but when he ascended to the first floor he was much impressed by the spacious living-room, large enough, it seemed, to hold all the people of the parish. He admired the long table, with its massive legs, the substantial chairs, the great box-stove, a three-decker, the handsome dresser, with its rows of blue and white crockery; but most of all the great copper kettle that stood upon the stove and occupied fully half of the lower oven.

"*Mon Dieu*, Jean!" he exclaimed. "Where did you get that kettle? Solid copper, as I live, and polished like a mirror. Truly, it is a treasure. They do not make such kettles now-a-days. An heirloom, no doubt."

"I am glad that you like it," said Jean, "for you are a judge of such things. The first Giroux brought it from Normandy in the days of Frontenac. Yes, it is an historic relic, I am told."

"No doubt, Jean, no doubt. The Giroux were notables in their day. My great-grandmother was of that family, and I am proud of it. We are cousins, you see. But that kettle—what changes it has seen! How many generations have come and gone since first it hung above the hearth-stone of the family Giroux! Think, my son, how much it has contributed to the happiness of all these generations. What potatoes, what soup, what ragout, what *compôte* of strawberries, raspberries, currants, what cherry cordial, what good things of every description have been prepared in that kettle! Times and customs change, but the old copper kettle goes on for ever. Ah, Jean, if I had served my generation like that I should not have lived in vain. Permit me to bless the ancient heir-loom and to wish that it may serve the family Giroux for many generations to come. There, my friend, was not that a good sermon upon a kettle?"

"Truly, Monsieur Paradis, you are a poet, who sees in the common things of life a meaning hidden to the vulgar eye. I shall love the old kettle more than ever after what you have said. But let us go up to the second floor, Monsieur, and after that to the roof. From that point one gets a view that is well worth the climb."

"What a view!" exclaimed Father Paradis, as he stood at last on the railed terrace that crowned the roof. "Your house, Jean, is very fine, one of the grandest that I have seen, but this panorama is magnificent, superb. How lovely the river, there below, winding through the valley like a thread of silver! How beautiful the cultivated fields, the rich meadows, the upland pastures, the peaceful homes beside the pleasant country road! How far-away everything looks, and how the lines and colours blend in the mellow evening light! How wonderful the forest surrounding all, and the mountains rising peak beyond peak to the very sky! The shadows cover the lower hills, but the high summits still glow in the last radiance of the setting sun. And those clouds that float far above in the blue ether, what robes of glory they wear, like angels doing homage before Him that sitteth upon the throne! Jean, Jean! It is the work of the good God. 'All thy works shall praise thee, O God, and thy saints shall bless thee!'"

Jean made no reply, and for a long time the two friends stood there in silence, the old man with the frail body and the silver hair, and the tall, strong, dark-haired man in all the pride and confidence of youth, their eyes filled with the glory of the sunset and their hearts with the beauty of the world. Presently the brightness faded from the mountain-top, the gold and crimson from the sky, and a white mist, stealing up the valley, covered everything as with a shroud. Father Paradis shuddered, as at the approach of death.

"There, Jean," he said with a sigh, "the day is done, dead, one might say. A blaze of light, a moment of brightness, and then the shadow. Ah, my son, 'thus passeth away the glory of the world!'"

"But, my father," said the young man, "to-morrow will be a new day, and meanwhile we shall have the moon and the stars. It is the first quarter of the moon now, and you will see her, a thin crescent over the western hill, when the mist has passed. There, look! How beautiful! Encouraging, is it not, to see the light again, though it be only a reflection? The sun, at least, is not extinguished, my father."

"No, Jean, that is true; yet I had almost forgotten it, I who should always hear the voice of God. Ah, my son, why did you not become a priest? How gladly would I have seen you stand in my place, between the living God and dying men! Jean, I think, as I have always thought, that you have a vocation and a message."

"It may be so," said Jean, after a pause. "But what is the vocation? What is the message? Not that which you think, my father, not at all. Look! I have seen my people, the habitants, toiling from morning to night, summer and winter, from year to year, like their fathers for many generations, and for what reward? Food and clothes and shelter, the bare necessaries of life, and all of the poorest kind. It is a living, perhaps, but it is not to live; and I say—it is my message, if you like—that for all their toil there should be more reward. The young men, my old playmates, say the same, and go away, to the States, to the North-West, and leave this land, this good land, to the old people and those without ambition, without enterprise. Monsieur Paradis, it is not well; it is not right. Some must go, no doubt, for the desire to wander is in the blood, but there should be place for those who would be glad to stay. Yes, here in St. Placide, in these beautiful mountains, by that lovely river. See, how it shines down there, in the light of the moon. It is a river to love, is it not, my father?"

"Jean," said the old man, in a sorrowful voice, "you also are an orator, a poet. There was a time when I, too, could talk like that. The enthusiasm of youth, how fine it is! But with age comes wisdom, born of experience. Now I know that poverty, which you deplore, is a good, and not an evil; and that wealth, which you desire for all, is a snare, a delusion. The poor are close to God, but the rich are often far from Him. It is the last thing that I would desire for the people of St. Placide, that they should increase in riches, for they would forget God. Yes, Jean, the good God loves the poor, and they cling to Him as their only hope. Our divine Saviour Himself was one of the very poor, and it is well to be like Him."

"Monsieur Paradis," said Jean, earnestly, "will you permit me to confess to you, not as to a priest, but as to an old and dear friend? I confess, my father, with sorrow but without repentance, that I disagree with you profoundly, absolutely. The Lord Jesus was poor, as you have said, but He had friends among the rich, who gave Him food and shelter, and, at the last, provided Him a tomb. No, my father, poverty in itself is not a good but an evil, one of the worst, and the cause of many others. Poverty, disease, ignorance, vice, crime — they all go together very often, yes, generally. It is not among the very rich, perhaps, that one finds the best citizens, but certainly not among the very poor. It is not great riches that I demand for the habitants of St. Placide, but better food and shelter, more suitable clothes, education, books, newspapers, art, science, amusement. At last we are awaking from our mediæval slumber. Civilization we must have, through the Church, if possible, but if not we must look elsewhere for the guidance, the leadership that we need. There, Monsieur, I have said more than I should, perhaps, but it was from the heart."

"Ah, Jean," said the old priest, with a sigh, " you have gone far. I had no idea that you were thinking such things during all the years since I first noticed you at the parish school. Education, civilization, prosperity —what can they do for us? It is not by prosperity, so-called, that you can make the people willing to stay on the land, to endure the hardships of habitant life. It is poverty, aided by religion, that can accomplish this miracle. Jean, you are too far advanced for St. Placide. Education, which you glorify, has unfitted you for our simple life, and that which you plan, with all the enthusiasm and ignorance of youth, can only end in failure and disaster. The revolutionist can do nothing here. Jean, my son, I had high hopes for you, but now I fear that you have not only strayed from the ways of the fathers, but that you have become alienated from the Holy Church, that you have forsaken God. It is some weeks since you have assisted at the Mass, and you have not come to confession for a long time. My son, there is to be a retreat of three days, beginning to-morrow, in honour of the Precious Blood. Will you not come with us, to meditate, to pray? You are busy, I know, but three days are not long compared with eternity, and the affairs of this life are trivial, after all. Say that you will come, Jean, my son."

"I cannot, Monsieur, for I have engagements that I must not break. Later I will come, for I am still a true son of the Church, and I have faith in God. But I have also faith in man, and believe——"

"Have faith in God, Jean. The heart of man is not to be trusted. Look to God, my son."

"I will," said Jean, with humility, "and for that reason I ask the blessing of God, and yours, my father, upon me and my poor house. Your blessing, Father Paradis. You cannot deny me."

"Jean," said the old man, "I fear for you; yet I know that you desire to do good, and I wish that you may have peace in your soul. 'Except the Lord build the house they labour in vain that build it.' May God bless you, my son, and may the work of your hands be established and be for the glory of God. Amen!"

Thus Father Paradis blessed the new house, although with misgivings, but many of the neighbours bore Jean no good will and freely expressed their disapproval of the hazardous and presumptuous undertaking. They came to the house-warming, as a matter of course, ate and drank of the abundant refreshments provided by Jean and his good mother, enjoyed the dance on the great kitchen floor, and then went home to criticize and prophesy evil. Even the best friends of the family allowed themselves to gossip on the subject, and did not disdain to stop at the crossroads to hear the latest news from Mère Tabeau, and her spicy comments thereon.

"Certainly, I was there," said she to one of the passers-by. "I was invited with the rest, of course. They do not love me, those Giroux, but they would not offer me an open insult. They would not dare. And I went, of course, to show my appreciation of the courtesy. I understand the art of politeness, as you know.

"What did I see? Why, Monsieur Gagnon, you were there yourself. I saw what you saw, my friend. For example, I saw a certain neighbour of mine drink fifteen cups of spruce beer and consume an equal number of *croquignoles*, one to each cup of beer, the right proportion, exactly. No, my good neighbour, I did not say it was you, but if the cap fits——

"What did I think of it all? Well, I have my thoughts, naturally. Shall I tell you, or are you in a hurry to go to market? No, for you have started an hour earlier than usual. Well, if you have patience to listen to an old woman, I will tell you. As to the affair of last evening, it was pleasant for the neighbours to be thus entertained. The money of Bonhomme Laroche was well spent. The Giroux will pay later, in the course of time ; yes, sooner than you think, perhaps.

"The house ? Oh, it is wonderful, by far the finest in the parish. Indeed, there is not the like in all Beauport. Only in the great city of Quebec can one see hotels like that. Twelve rooms! *Mon Dieu!* Where are all the people who will occupy them ? How long will they stay ? How much will they pay ? These are important questions, as you can see. Figure to yourself. If there were twenty tourists in the house for two months, that is, for the whole summer, and if the foolish people paid as much as four dollars a week, a great sum for these parts, that would be only a little more than six hundred dollars. There is no great fortune in that. A considerable sum in the gross, but the net revenue will be very small. When you have taken interest on the loan, the cost of food, the wages of Pauline La Chance, the hired girl, and all the other expenses, what will be left to pay for the work of Madame Giroux and Jean himself, not to mention a thousand little items, of no account in themselves but great in the aggregate. Oh, I know arithmetic, I assure you, as well as many other things. It is useful, at times, to be able to count. Figures, at least, do not lie.

"What will happen ? That is not hard to tell. Even you, Monsieur Gagnon, could look into the future on those terms. When the expenses exceed the income, what takes place ? One pays out all one's ready money, one borrows, sells a cow, a horse, a piece of land. But there comes an end to all that, and then the notice at the Church door, the sale, the farewell, the departure, the talk for a while, and after that all is forgotten. They are gone. Whither? Who knows? Who cares? Only old gossips like me remember. Only good friends like me know or care.

"The house has no name as yet. Well, I will give it one. I will call it *La Folie Giroux.* As you have heard, fools build houses, but wise men live in them. It is Bonhomme Laroche who is the wise man in this case. But it may be that Jean Baptiste will become wise. Who can tell? Bonhomme Laroche has a daughter, you know.

"But I must stop, neighbour Gagnon, or you will think that I must be paid for my talk. But I am only a poor old woman who likes to see the neighbours as they pass. It is my only pastime. And the good neighbours are very kind to me. Only yesterday Bonhomme Bédard gave me a fine bag of flour, enough to last for three months. He is not a rich man, by any means, but very generous. If only I had a few potatoes, now. Oh, no, Monsieur Gagnon, it is too charitable of you. A whole sack! It is too much. If you had given me a dozen of those fine trout it would have been enough. Those too? Monsieur Gagnon, God will prosper you. *Au revoir,* my dear friend. Good luck to you."

When Jean Baptiste heard that Mère Tabeau had given his new house a name, he laughed and said that she was very kind to save him the trouble, that all men were fools and all the works of man monuments of folly. So he painted the name in large black letters above the door—LA FOLIE. Most of the neighbours took it as a joke, but some shook their heads in dismay and crossed themselves repeatedly as they passed by.

It was unlucky, they said, to give a bad name to a house or a child. One should invoke the protection of Heaven, rather, of the Holy Virgin or of one of the saints. As to the old witch, Mère Tabeau, one should have nothing to do with her, for she was in league with Satan.

CHAPTER XII

PROFIT AND LOSS

THE summer tourist, more than other men, is a confirmed egoist. Sincerely believing himself the centre of the universe and the chief end of all creation, he views with satisfaction the successful efforts of men and things to minister unto him. Hotels and boarding-houses exist for him; for him horses and carriages of every kind, with their obliging drivers, move to and fro; for him spring chickens cheerfully die; for him the sun shines by day, the moon by night, and the Aurora shimmers in the northern sky. How good God is to the summer tourist!

But there is the point of view of another egoist, the pious habitant of Murray Bay, Cacouna, Tadoussac, and all the other watering-places below Quebec. The good God loves the faithful. He sends rain in summer, snow in winter, and all the changes of weather in their season. He sends the birds of the air—the partridge, the wild duck and the brant. He sends the fishes of the great river—the eel, the sturgeon and the salmon; the trout, also, of the smaller lakes and rivers. He provides game in the forest—the red deer, the caribou, the moose, and all fur-bearing animals. He gives the strawberry, the raspberry, the blueberry, spruce gum, balsam, sarsaparilla and gold-thread. All these the good God provides, but, best of all, he sends the summer tourist to pour the wealth of the city into the lap of the habitant. Truly, it would be ungrateful and impious not to make the most of such an opportunity, not to exploit and cultivate in the most approved way that most profitable of crops—the summer tourist.

Jean Baptiste was a habitant by ten generations of thrifty ancestors, and could see, as well as any man, the possibilities of the summer tourist. He loved the genial egoist for his own sake, but more for the golden harvest that he should yield. For him he had built the great house; for him he had provided bed and board, horses and vehicles, canoes and guides, both indoor and outdoor games—all at great cost and no little risk—but to what end? Surely not for the good of the tourist alone, but that he might lay deep and broad the foundations of his own fortune, that he might begin and carry on the great works of which he dreamed by night and day.

Was it a vocation, as Father Paradis had said, and had he a message to deliver? Yes, there was a call, both loud and clear, and a message had been given him—to proclaim the gospel of the new era, to be the forerunner of the economic salvation of his people. A voice, he was, in the wilderness, crying: " Prepare ye the way of the Lord ! "—along the valley, by the river, over the mountain, to make the crooked ways straight, the rough places plain, to overcome every obstacle, every stumbling-block, until all men should get a vision of the future that was theirs, and rise up and possess the land. " It is my work," said Jean to himself. " It is also the work of God."

Jean was a prophet, like his great patron saint, a dreamer, one who had heard the voice of God in the silence of the wilderness, and was going forth to declare the vision and proclaim the word to those who had eyes to see and ears to hear. The great idea filled his mind, and he believed himself devoted heart and soul to the cause which he had espoused, for the good of man and the glory of God. Yet as he looked into the depths of his own heart, as one gazing into a crystal, he saw there another image enshrined, and he began to doubt and to wonder whether he were the servant of a divine ideal or the slave of an alluring earthly love. Was it possible that he had not yet seen the vision that compels, had not yet heard the silence that takes control ?

Jean freely admitted to himself that he loved Gabrielle. Who could help it ? Who would not admire that lithe, graceful figure, with the springing step and free toss of the head, like a wild deer of the forest ? Who would not rejoice to see that glorious hair ? Who could gaze unmoved upon that lovely face and form ? Who would not desire to take her to his arms—his very own ? But how proud and cold at times ! How those blue eyes could glitter like steel ! How those laughing, tantalizing lips could curve in bitter scorn ! How that beautiful creature, with all the charms of woman since the days of Eve, could with every glance, every tone, every gesture flaunt the flag of no-surrender ! The challenge must be accepted ; the defiance could not be endured.

More than that—in all Jean's work, in all his thoughts and plans Gabrielle was a part. When he crossed the little bridge over La Branche—it was there that he first noticed Gabrielle's reddish-golden hair. When he was by the river—it was there that he had met her tripping over the stones in her short skirt and high boots, with rod and creel, a fisher-maiden whom more than fish might fear. When he passed through the woods, he saw her sitting under the trees amid patches of golden sunshine. When he was in church, she was kneeling there in prayer; and when he gazed at the high altar it was a glorified vision of Gabrielle that he saw, and not the Mother of God. When he thought of his great house, Gabrielle was there; on the day of triumph she would be his wife, his queen; and if ever misfortune came, he would go forth joyously to face the world, if only she were by his side.

Yet Jean believed that Gabrielle was not first in his heart. His work, his vocation, commanded obedience above all. War first; then love. Achievement, victory; then the crown and the reward. True, she might not consent to take the second place in his scheme of life. Women were by nature jealous, unreasonable, demanding more than man could give. She might be angry when she discovered the order of precedence. Poor little Gabrielle! She might go to a nunnery, even, as many young girls did when they could not have their own way, or when they saw the vanity of the world. That would be a pity. No, he would never allow that. What were the stone walls of a convent compared with the power of love? But she might love another man. Ah, that was different. Where was that other who dared to raise his eyes to Gabrielle? Where? Who?

At the very thought Jean's eyes flashed beneath his lowered eyebrows; his jaw set; his hands clenched; and his figure rose to its full height, bending forward with such menace as would have given pause to any rival who dared to contend for the prize of love with Jean Baptiste Giroux.

But it was only a girl that met him at the turn of the

road, a girl with waving hair and laughing eyes—the girl of his dreams.

"*Mon Dieu*, Jean!" said Gabrielle, in a tantalizing voice, before he had time to speak. "How fierce you look! I am almost afraid to be walking here alone, on the king's highway. Is the thought of me so terrifying? I am quite harmless, I assure you. Or are you thinking of the last time we met, when I was so cross? I was provoked, you know, but I have got over it. It is hard to be cross with you, Jean."

"Is it?" said Jean, simply. "I thought it was quite easy, much too easy, in fact."

"Ah, stupid!" said Gabrielle, with a laugh. "All men are stupid, I think, and you more than others. How is it that you are so dull, Jean?"

"Gabrielle," said Jean, meditatively, "am I really dull? I did not know it. At school I was thought rather clever. As for books——"

"Ah, bah!" said Gabrielle, with scorn. "Talk to me of books—what does one learn from them? Mere stupidities, that is all."

"But," persisted Jean, "there are other things that I can do, where the stupidity of which you speak does not show itself so much. For example——"

"For example!" said Gabrielle, in a mocking voice. "For example! Tell me, do!"

"I forget," said Jean.

"Ha! Ha!" laughed Gabrielle, in glee. "What did I say? He forgets, the silly one, forgets all his reading, spelling, arithmetic, his Latin and Greek and Hebrew—all his knowledge. Well, let me remind you, Jean, that you are one of those paragons who can do everything. Not only have you all the knowledge of the world, but you have facilities which mere scholars do not possess. You hunt, you fish, you trap—like an Indian. You run like a deer, jump like a grasshopper, swim like a fish, fly like a bird, almost. Oh, I am sure that you could fly, if you tried. Try once; please do, just for my sake. But to forget all that, and more! How did you succeed in forgetting so much, Jean, my friend?"

" It was when I saw you, Gabrielle."

" Me!" gasped Gabrielle. " What have I done?"

" Nothing, Gabrielle. Yes, everything; for you have stolen my heart."

" Your heart, Jean? Impossible! That is what does not exist. A great strong body? Yes. A brain? Certainly. Capacity of every kind? Oh, yes. But a heart? Do not deceive yourself. You have no heart to lose. No, no! Do not touch me! Do not dare! But answer! Is it not as I have said?"

" It may be so, Gabrielle; but when will you marry me, dear?"

" What is that you say? Marry you? Oh, no; I could not."

" Why not, Gabrielle? Why not, little one?"

" Oh, there are many, many reasons. In the first place, I do not love you, Jean."

" That is because you will not let yourself love me, Gabrielle."

" Again, Jean, you do not love me."

" How do you know, Gabrielle?"

" You have never told me."

" Gabrielle, listen to me——"

" No, no; I will not. You would deceive me with your talk, great Jesuit that you are. Let me speak.

I say that you love no one, Jean Baptiste Giroux. It is your great house that you love, your horses and cattle, your barns, your precious tourists. There is your treasure; there is your heart, Jean Baptiste."

"Oh, Gabrielle, what are those things compared with you? They are nothing, nothing."

"Jean, my friend, I like to hear you say that. Say it again, Jean."

"Gabrielle, what are houses, barns, lands, and all that, compared with my love for you? I love you, dear; and if I value those things it is for your sake. They are all for you. I lay them at your feet, and myself as well."

"Do you mean it? Do you really mean what you say?"

"Yes, Gabrielle."

"Well, Jean, I will take you at your word. That house of yours—I hate it. Those tourists, those people who walk about staring at everybody—I detest them. How could you bring them here to spoil the peace and joy of our lovely valley, to change our ancestral ways, to turn everything upside down? But we will send them away, back to Quebec, to Montreal, to Pittsburg, never to return, and everything will be as before. Yes, they shall go home, and the house we will dedicate to another purpose."

"Gabrielle," said Jean, earnestly, "why did you not tell me this before—a year ago? Now it is too late."

"Too late? Why, then, if you love me as you say?"

"Because I have embarked on this enterprise after much thought and long deliberation. I have put into it my strength of body and brain, my property, my life, my honour—and it is too late to turn back. The ship is laden, the anchor weighed, and we have put out to sea with a fair wind. Return to harbour? By no means. You do not ask it, Gabrielle."

"There," said Gabrielle, with a sob, "what did I tell you? You do not love me. It is yourself that you love, Jean, and all those stupid plans of yours."

"But no, Gabrielle, all are for you, as the means to the end. How can one have the end without the means?"

"Oh, I could tell you very well, but I will not. It is easy to see that you have made up your mind. Well, there is another who has a mind of her own. Adieu, Monsieur. Here our paths divide. Take the broad, dusty road, if you like. For me, I take this little path through the woods—alone. No, you shall not."

"Gabrielle, this is most unfair, cruel, heartless."

"It may be so, but I know another who is cruel, who has no heart—it is Monseigneur Jean Baptiste Giroux."

With this she went away through the woods, humming a song about a gay, inconstant lover, quite different from Jean Baptiste:

> "Papillon, tu es volage !
> Tu ressembl' à mon amant.
> L'amour est un badinage,
> L'amour est un passe-temps,
> Quand j'ai mon amant
> J'ai le cœur content."

CHAPTER XIII

THE RETURN OF PAMPHILE

"AH, there is mine host of La Folie," said Mère Tabeau, in a loud voice, as Jean, in a brown study, dead to the world, was passing her place on his way home.

"Jean, Jean Baptiste!" she called, but still he gave no heed.

"Monsieur Jean, Monsieur Jean Baptiste, Monsieur Giroux, Monseigneur! Why the deuce does not his lordship stop? I must run after him, I see."

The old woman, with surprising agility, ran after Jean, plucked him by the sleeve, and immediately resumed her cringing attitude, leaning heavily upon her staff.

"There he goes," she whined. "His lordship does not see his old friends, does not hear them, even, when they speak."

"Oh, pardon me, Madame Tabeau," said Jean, politely. "I was seeing nothing, hearing nothing. Of late I have become absent-minded, I think."

"Quite natural," said Mère Tabeau. "The very young are absent-minded, and the very old, but also those who are immersed in affairs and those who are in love. They are most absorbing, those affairs of the heart. I remember well my last case, now many years ago. Some day I will tell you the story. Perhaps you could listen to it now."

"But no, Madame. I am in haste this evening.

Another time, if you please. You had something else to say, had you not?"

"Not at all, Monseigneur. The poor old woman has nothing to say—nothing. Another time, when his lordship has a few minutes to spare for such trifles—his own affairs, moreover—I will wait upon him."

"Oh, Madame, do not be angry. I will listen, to be sure, all the afternoon, if I can be of service to you."

"Service to yourself, my friend. But no matter. I accept your apologies. I am well disposed, as you will see, and I wish to help you out of your troubles."

"My troubles?" said Jean, with a puzzled frown. "I do not understand. You speak in mysterious language, it seems. All of us have our little troubles, I suppose."

"Monsieur does not understand—will not, rather. Mysterious? Not at all. Does not everybody know that Monsieur Giroux would effect an alliance with one of the most prominent families in the parish? Is it possible that he has not yet heard what is common report?"

"Madame Tabeau, if that is all I had better go. I am really very busy."

"But, but, Monsieur, these affairs can be arranged, no matter how complicated, involved, entangled. I have charms, herbs, love potions, and all that, and there are other means still more efficacious. Besides, my charges are very moderate, a little commission, a mere bagatelle when compared with a dowry so magnificent, a connection so advantageous. If Mademoiselle——"

"Madame, that will do. The neighbours may gossip, if they please, but I will not. Allow me to leave you at this time."

"Go then, stupid! *Sacrée tête de mouton!* The fool will not listen. Well, he will suffer, he will pay; and I will offer my services to some one else. His lordship is not the only eligible young man in the parish of St. Placide."

"If that is all, Madame, I bid you good evening."

"No, there is something else. My friend, do not mind the ravings of an old woman, an old, old woman, poor and infirm. Old people like to talk, as you know, and say more than they should, at times. But it is their only pleasure. When one talks to a good listener like yourself one forgets. It is good to forget, Jean, to extinguish the fires of memory, if only for a moment. It is like a cup of cold water to a soul in purgatory."

"Madame."

"Yes, yes, I know. You are sorry for me, but not as I am sorry for myself. When I think of what I might have been and what I am, I could cry—and curse. But let us change the subject. You remember my nephew, Pamphile Lareau, do you not? A playmate of yours, I believe, some years ago."

"Remember Pamphile? Certainly. But I did not know that he was your nephew."

"You do not know everything, Jean, wise as you are. Pamphile is my nephew, as I have said, although I have never seen him. His mother thought herself more respectable than I. Can you believe it? After her death I came to St. Placide. For what purpose? Ah, that is my affair. You do not know that either, Monsieur the scholar. There is a lot of useful information that you do not obtain from books, I assure you. But Pamphile is coming to see me this very day. Do you see that little cloud of dust down the road? It is he, I am sure. Wait a moment and you will see him."

"That will be interesting," said Jean. "He has changed much, no doubt, in all these years."

"No doubt. He also has become a great lord, evidently. See, he comes in great style, in a carriage, all the way from Quebec. It will cost at least five dollars, that equipage, for so long a drive. Where the deuce did my nephew get all that money? He never sent me any of it. He will give some to his poor old aunt before he leaves, let us hope. There, he arrives. *Dieu*, what a dash! What grandeur! Speak to him, Jean, I cannot."

"*Bonjour*, Madame. *Bonjour*, Monsieur," said an imposing personage, as the carriage pulled up suddenly in a cloud of dust. "It is here, is it not, that Madame Tabeau lives? They told me, there below, that I should find the place at the crossroads."

"It is here, Monsieur," said Madame Tabeau, quite humbly. "If Monsieur will be so kind as to alight."

"With the greatest pleasure, Madame. How good it is to come to the end of a drive of four hours! Yes, four hours and ten minutes, by the watch. It is now four o'clock, is it not, Monsieur?"

"By the sun I should call it six o'clock, at least," said Jean. "You see, Monsieur the stranger, that we do not carry gold watches in St. Placide."

"No, to be sure. I had forgotten. A primitive place, truly. Is it possible that I spent my early years in St. Placide? But six o'clock? Surely not. Ah, I have it. Ha! Ha! How curious! It is that I have not set my watch since I left Elko, and there is a difference of two hours—or is it three?"

"Two hours," said Jean, with confidence. "You have mountain time there, I believe, and here we have eastern time. Yes, two hours."

The stranger's eyes narrowed as he looked sharply at Jean.

"Eh, what ? You know that ? What the deuce ? Who is this ? The little priest, as I live ! Monseigneur ! And as learned as ever, always wishing to teach one something, always casting away pearls of knowledge. Well met, my ancient friend, after all these years. This is too much pleasure. Your hand, my brave one, for the sake of old times."

The stranger extended a long, slender hand that closed about Jean's fingers like a vice of steel ; but Jean understood the trick of the thumb as well as he, and it was Pamphile's hand that was the first to relax.

"Enough, enough, my brave one. It is the same Jean Baptiste that I see and feel. *Dieu*, but you have a loving clasp of the hand. It brings tears to the eyes. Well, my friend the cabby, you seem impatient. What can I do for you ? "

"My fare, if you please, Monsieur—the little five dollars that we spoke of."

"Ah, yes, assuredly," said Pamphile, drawing out of his pocket a roll of bills, not one of a lower denomination than twenty dollars. "You can change American money, no doubt."

"Certainly, Monsieur. Anything less than twenty dollars."

"Not twenty dollars, cabby ? What a country ! We are not in Nevada, evidently. Well, my friend, this is unfortunate. What are we to do ? "

"I will take the twenty dollars, Monsieur."

"You will take it all, my friend? How good of you! *Sacré!* I have a mind to give it to you as a reward of merit. It is seldom that one meets a cabby so obliging, so resourceful. You will go far, my Jehu. Yes, I am thinking of giving you the twenty dollars. Do you still feel that you could accept it?"

"No, no, Monsieur," broke in Mère Tabeau. "*Mon Dieu*, what would you do? Give him twenty dollars? Two dollars and fifty cents would have been quite enough if only you had made a bargain. What can we do? Let us think. I could perhaps find the money. Yes, Monsieur Giroux, I have a little store laid by, even I, for my funeral. Wait a moment. I will get it at once."

In her excitement Mère Tabeau forgot both rheumatism and stick, as one who had been cured at the shrine of Bonne Ste. Anne, ran into the house and presently returned with a little leathern bag, out of which she counted silver and copper coins until the cabby had a handful of small change equal to the amount of his fare.

"That is a bad penny, Madame," said the cabby, returning a much-worn coin.

"But no, it is perfectly good, perfectly good," said the old woman, angrily. "It goes, I tell you. I received it, did I not? Well, you shall take it in your turn, and if you don't like it you may pass it on. No, not another *sou*. You are a shark, a robber!"

"Let him have another, Madame," drawled Pamphile with a grand air. "Give him his five dollars in full and a quarter for drink. The twenty-dollar bill? Oh, it is back in my pocket. To-morrow we will arrange all that. And you are Madame Tabeau, no doubt, the aunt whom I have never seen until this blessed moment.

Well, my aunt, it is a pleasure to meet you. But where is the little priest who was here a moment since?"

"He is gone, Monsieur Lareau. His lordship has marched away. He would not wait the pleasure of any man. Rich habitants, notaries, priests, bishops, American millionaires—they are all the same to him. It is a great lord, that. One cannot but admire him for his strength, his capacity, but I should like, I should like to slap him in the face."

"And I," drawled Pamphile, "I should like to meet him in Elko, Nevada, in the middle of the street, at twenty paces, or forty, even. Cric! Crac! Jean Baptiste falls in the dust, and there is one monseigneur less in the world. But that would not do in St. Placide, perhaps."

"For the love of God, Monsieur, do not speak so loud. Come into the house, if you please, where we can talk. Enter, Monsieur. It is not a palace, nor is it a hovel, altogether. See, all is very proper—the dining-room and kitchen in one, the sleeping apartment of Monsieur over there in the corner, and my own little boudoir in the attic. No, Monsieur, do not fear to be alone with an old woman like me. There was a time— but let us not speak of it. It is past, the golden age, and now there is nothing but rheumatism, broken bones, and the hobble to the grave.

"But before that one may have some pleasure still. One may gossip with the neighbours as they pass, frighten the women and the children, tell a few lies now and then, and, best of all, one may have revenge. Yes, life is worth living yet. We will live for that, you and I. You also have your little scores to pay, it would seem. How glad I am that you have come! What luck! But how did it happen that you left Nevada, Monsieur my nephew?"

"Oh, a little unpleasantness," said Pamphile, evasively. "One cannot stay always in the same place. One outlives one's usefulness. So it occurred to me that I might visit the scenes of my childhood, and when your letter came I decided to take a change and a rest, for the good of my health."

"And a little adventure as well," said Mère Tabeau, significantly. "A little expedition in search of gold, perhaps."

"Possibly," said Pamphile, with a smile, "if it could easily be done and without danger."

"Monsieur my nephew, listen to me. Directly east from this spot, through the forest and beyond the mountain, ten miles as the crow flies but twenty by the road, lies the village of Chateau Richer, where I was born many years ago—yes, more than sixty years. It was there that I passed my early years, and when I arrived at the age of love I was there still, in my little house by the shore, where I could see the bateaux pass up the river with the rising tide and pass down again with the ebb.

"Did the sailors stop sometimes on the way? Possibly. At least the smugglers came to see my brother Ovide. They were brave people, those smugglers, and rich as well. There were two who had a great treasure, obtained from the trade, in part, but chiefly from a wreck. They were wreckers too, of course. When the good God sends a storm, when a ship runs on the rocks, when all on board are drowned, does not the wreck belong to those who find it? Assuredly. So Michel Gamache and Toussaint Giroux found the

THE RETURN OF PAMPHILE

wreck and the treasure on Anticosti, there below. They burned the wreck, brought the treasure home to the island, and hid it in a cave in the side of the hill by the long marsh.

"How do I know? Did I not see it on that night when Michel rowed me across the river at high tide when the moon was full. What a night it was! How bright the moon shone in the sky and in the still water beneath! How the grass rustled under the keel of the boat as we ran up into the little cove! I can hear it still. How dark it was in that cave, but how the gold coins glistened! Yes, gold coins, Napoleons, sovereigns, hundreds of them, in an iron box. Heavy? I could not lift it. Of what value? How should I know? Ten, twenty, thirty thousand pounds, perhaps. Oh, a great treasure. See, there is one of those coins, a love token which he gave me, he, Michel Gamache, and which I keep until the day of reckoning. I have a grudge against him? Yes, a little grudge, a slight affair of the heart which I have nourished for some forty years, for which I would kill him if I could be sure that he would go to the place of eternal fire."

"Well, my aunt," said Pamphile, with a yawn, "it is a fine story, but to what purpose? Was it to tell me this that you brought me from Elko?"

"But no, my nephew. Do you not know that Michel Gamache lives in this parish?"

"No."

"And the treasure, I tell you, those Napoleons and sovereigns, all that gold, is here in St. Placide, in the same iron box, of a weight more than you could lift, my strong nephew. No, you could do it, with some assistance, and that is why I have asked you to come.

Eh, Pamphile, would not an adventure like this be as good as gambling in Nevada? Not so amusing, perhaps, but quite as profitable."

"Quite so, my aunt. And where, if I may ask, is this wonderful treasure to be found?"

"All in good time, my nephew, when everything is arranged. You will help me, will you not? We will divide the spoils. You shall have two-thirds of the treasure. I shall have the rest, and my revenge. Are the terms satisfactory?"

"More than satisfactory, my dear aunt. And the little priest, what of him?"

"Oh, that will explain itself. You will get even with him very soon, never fear. It is my little secret for the present. Yes, a fine little secret. It will reveal itself before long. If not, I will tell you."

"My aunt," said Pamphile, impatiently, "I don't give a hoot for your little secret. Keep it to yourself as long as you like, but give me something to eat."

"Well! well! Such are men — always eating. Nothing can satisfy them, neither gold, nor love, nor revenge—only meat, potatoes, soup and all that. Well, my nephew, I was expecting you, and presently we shall have a little repast together—soup of peas, fried trout, strawberries, cream, tea. How will that do? Ah, Pamphile, what a fine, tall man you are! What arms, shoulders, legs! More than a match for that Jean Baptiste, surely."

"No, my aunt; he is a giant, that little priest. My fingers tingle still from that grip of his. No, but I shall punish him all the same. There are other ways."

"Ha! Ha!" cackled the old crone, in glee. "There are other ways. Yes, indeed. Ah, my little secret, my dear little secret."

CHAPTER XIV

THE TRIUMPH OF PAMPHILE

It was on a Saturday evening that Pamphile arrived in St. Placide, and before Mass on the following morning all the parish knew that the exile had returned, not in poverty and rags, like the prodigal son, but with fine clothes on his back, money in his pocket, and driving in a carriage like a great lord. Some of the neighbours had merely heard of his arrival; others had seen him as he drove by; while a very few, highly favoured, had actually spoken to him; but on the way to Mass all the details were pieced together, the knowledge of each became the common property of all, and a story of adventure and romance was woven that grew more wonderful and variegated with the telling.

The youth had left the parish eight years before without a *sou*. Zotique Bédard himself had taken him down to Beauport as an act of charity; and Elzéar Buchon, the grocer's boy, had taken him the rest of the way to Quebec. From that place he had made his way, by walking, by getting a lift now and then, by riding in and under freight cars, to Chicago, and finally to the Far West, where for many years he had wandered about from one mining camp to another seeking for gold, now finding a glittering vein that promised a fortune, now losing all at a single blast. At last he had found it, a mine of fabulous riches, and now he was a capitalist, a millionaire, living on rents and royalties, travelling for pleasure all over the world, yet coming back, like a good patriot, to the home of his ancestors.

As to his wealth there could be no doubt whatever. One had but to look at the fine frock coat of grey cloth, the embroidered waistcoat, the striped trousers, the shiny buttoned shoes, and the jaunty grey hat of soft felt with the silken cord and tassel. Such style St. Placide had never seen before, and Quebec, even, could not approach it. The housewives marvelled at the whiteness of his shirt-bosom; the young men talked of the glittering diamond stud and the gold watch with its wonderful hunting-case and the little gong within that chimed the hours; while the young ladies raved over his drooping moustache and the black, glossy mane that came down almost to his shoulders.

Altogether, the verdict was highly favourable. Pamphile was a desirable young man, a credit to the parish. What a pity that he had not come back to stay! But it was not to be expected that he could be content to settle down in St. Placide, he who had travelled over the world and had attained such eminence among his fellow-men. No, but it might well be that he had returned to seek a bride among the fair maidens of the parish. Riches might be acquired abroad, but more loving companions, more faithful wives or better housekeepers than the Canadian girls were not to be found in foreign lands. *Vive la Canadienne!*

True, Pamphile had not left behind a perfect reputation when he went away, but one should not be too severe in judging the pranks and peccadilloes of youth. The worst boys often become the best men. In fact, some of the most respectable habitants had been sad rogues in their younger days. No, a boy without capacity for evil had little capacity for good. It is not enough to be good ; one must be good for something.

Of the relatives of Pamphile little was known. His mother had been the sister of Mère Tabeau, but was now dead. His father had been a lumberman on the Gatineau, but was drowned on the drive. Of the dead one should say nothing but good. The family was by no means distinguished, but that was all the more to the credit of Pamphile, who had been able to rise so far above them. And Mère Tabeau ? Well, after all she was a harmless creature, despite her bitter tongue. Certainly, she had a gift of language truly remarkable. If only she had a silk dress, a black cloak, and a bonnet tied with ribbons under her chin, she would look quite respectable. Indeed, the wives of some of the habitants had a loud voice and an offensive manner. One must not be unjust to people merely because they are poor.

So the neighbours, as they drove to Church, praised the achievements of Pamphile and said many charitable things of Mère Tabeau. More than one stopped at the cabin to invite the old woman and her distinguished nephew to drive to Church with them. The first to come was Bonhomme Gagnon, who, after some delay, captured the lion and the lioness and bore them away in triumph. It was indeed a triumph for Bonhomme Gagnon, and fully repaid him for the gifts of trout, game, berries, potatoes, black puddings and what not, the blackmail extorted for years by Mère Tabeau because of a slight indiscretion in the days of his youth. Even Madame Gagnon, who cordially hated the old woman, condescended to sit with her in the back seat for the pleasure of escorting the American millionaire and mining king to church.

It was a great day for Pamphile. Seated beside the eminently respectable cultivator, Bonhomme Gagnon, he found himself at the head of a long procession of neighbours, assembled, it would seem, to do him honour. He thoroughly enjoyed the attention he was receiving, he who had been so unimportant in his younger days that the neighbours could hardly remember his faults, much less his good points, such as they were. But now the insignificant past was obliterated, the way of virtue and honour lay before him, and the rising sun of popular favour shone upon him. The heart of Pamphile expanded in the genial warmth of the morning sun, and he chatted in a very friendly way with the worthy habitant by his side.

"Well, Monsieur Gagnon," he said, in a tone of appreciation, "this is without doubt a very fine day."

The good habitant beamed upon Pamphile.

"I am delighted to hear you say so, Monsieur Lareau. You find our weather pleasant? That is good. Yes, we have fine weather at times, not like that of the West, of course, but still quite satisfactory. Good for the hay, certainly."

"Ah, Monsieur Gagnon, my friend, not only is the day very fine, but the scenery, I will say, is charming. Not like that of Nevada, but equally pleasing in its way."

"Can it be?" exclaimed Bonhomme Gagnon, delighted. "It is a pleasure to hear you say so, Monsieur. The weather and the scenery—both equal to Nevada in their way. But that is gratifying. Do you hear that, Marie? The gentleman has seen the world, and he knows. What a wonderful thing is travel! To go to Beauport, that is interesting; to visit Quebec, that is very fine; but to sail up to Montreal, to explore the sources of the great river, to see Chicago, Nevada and all that—what a privilege! Ah, Monsieur Lareau, I envy you."

"Yes, it is interesting," said Pamphile, reflectively. "But it is interesting, also, to return. St. Placide has changed much in the past eight years. Those good neighbours back there have an air of prosperity. Almost every one has a covered buggy. Formerly they had carts only, and many walked to Church, five, six, seven miles, even. Yes, St. Placide must be a pretty good place."

"Not so bad, Monsieur Lareau," said Bonhomme Gagnon, with pride. "There are no millionaires in our parish, but neither are there any paupers. Yes, we have our cows and pigs, our horses and spring-carts, our houses and barns, and our money in the bank. It is the dairy business, you know, that has made the change of which you speak. I myself, for example, have my little five hundred dollars laid away."

"That is interesting," said Pamphile, with a keen glance at the simple habitant. "Very interesting indeed. And you are contented I am sure, as though you owned a gold mine."

"Contented? Yes. No. A gold mine? *Mon Dieu*, if I had that I should be a prince. Marie, do not talk all the time. Listen to Monsieur Lareau, who will tell us, perhaps, about the gold of Nevada. Tell us, Monsieur, if you please. Is it true that one finds a mine, now and then, with more than a million dollars in gold, pure gold?"

"Certainly, Monsieur Gagnon. Have I not seen

with my own eyes that great mine, the Comstock, whence they have taken millions and millions of gold and silver, besides lead, copper, and many other metals of great value? Ah, that was a mine! Yes, there is gold in Nevada — quantities of it. Come with me, Monsieur Gagnon, on my return, and I will show you. My own little mine, for example, would be worth a visit. I could show you places on the wall of the tunnel where you could pick off pieces of gold as large as a pea—yes, as large as a marble. Native gold, pure, twenty dollars to the ounce."

"Monsieur Lareau, I will go with you. Marie, say nothing. Too old? Not at all. I was sixty last month, but what of that? I am strong still, as an ox. The farm? You will see to that. She is a most capable manager, Monsieur Lareau. Danger, you say? Indians? Highway robbers? I had not thought of that. I am no fighter, me, and I have no desire to lose my scalp. There is not much hair left, but I need it all. Tell us, Monsieur Lareau—is there really danger?"

"Oh, yes, a little danger, of course, enough to make life interesting, but we do not think of that. I carry a revolver, of course, and robbers do not often attack one who can hit a nail on the head at fifty yards. Yes, it demands a keen eye and a steady hand, such as one seldom has at the age of sixty. No, Monsieur Gagnon, perhaps you had better stay in St. Placide. But it is a pity, a great pity. A man with a little capital, like yourself, could make a fortune in a little while."

"But could not one send one's money?" inquired Bonhomme Gagnon, with great eagerness. "Could one not send it by a good friend like yourself, an old compatriot and neighbour? Marie, is it not the thing to do, to send that five hundred dollars by Monsieur Lareau, and to receive, say, half of the profits? A species of partnership, that. If only you would, Monsieur."

"No, no, Monsieur Gagnon, I could not. Five hundred dollars is a small sum in Nevada. In the mining of gold one requires ten times as much, and after that there may be need of more. No, let us not speak of it. It would not be worth while."

"But Monsieur Lareau," persisted the old man, now afire with the gold fever, "behold the neighbours back there, each with his little store in the bank, or in some other safe place, his two hundred, five hundred, one thousand dollars, even. Then there is that rich Bonhomme Laroche, to whom a thousand dollars is nothing; and Monsieur Taché, who is a lumber king, almost. Do not refuse us, Monsieur Lareau. Consider, if you please. We might easily raise as much as ten thousand dollars. That would be sufficient, would it not, to buy a little gold mine?"

"Monsieur Gagnon," said Pamphile, with an air of great sincerity, "I ask you to observe that I did not make the proposal, and that I advise you once more to be content with your little three per cent. in the Bank of Quebec. Still, if you insist, and if Madame approves, we may consider the matter. If you do not change your mind, come to see me during the week, and we will talk. Those who begin an enterprise like this, the promoters we call them, always have a certain advantage over the others whom we take into the company. We are on the ground floor, you know, at the beginning of things, and the others we take in above. Yourself, Monsieur Gagnon, to whom the idea first occurred, would have the precedence; then I; and after us the others in their turn. But as I have said, there is always the chance of loss. Yet the profits are alluring, and the search for gold, it draws one on. But let us not speak of it any more at present. Here we are at the church. What a crowd of people! Let us descend, Monsieur and Madame. Let us descend, my aunt. Yes, Monsieur Gagnon, we shall be charmed to drive back with you after Mass."

During the service, Pamphile and his aunt, who occupied a place well toward the front, were the centre of all eyes; and it is to be suspected that the thoughts, also, of the people were centred, not upon the worship of the good God, but upon the handsome stranger who was assisting at the service with a devotion that might have put even the churchwardens to shame. What would the neighbours have thought if they had known the thoughts of the pious stranger at the most solemn part of the office, when the priest was elevating the Host, and all the people bowed in awe and adoration? He was thinking of the last time that he had assisted at the holy sacrifice, when Jean Baptiste and he were acolytes, both eager to have the honour of ringing the little bell. It was Pamphile's turn on this occasion, but Jean twisted the bell out of his hand and robbed him of his sacred right. After this, as the acolytes knelt with folded hands behind the priest, Pamphile had said, through his clenched teeth: " For this I will kill you one day, Jean Baptiste Giroux."

Now, after many years, as the little bell announced the elevation of the *Bon Dieu*, Saviour of the world, Pamphile repeated with hate in his soul the same words: " For that I will kill you, Jean Baptiste Giroux."

THE TRIUMPH OF PAMPHILE

After Mass the neighbours flocked about Pamphile: those who had known him to take him by the hand, to welcome him back to the parish, and to remind him of old times: those who had not known him to look at the distinguished stranger, to listen to his talk, and to have the honour of an introduction. With a grand and gracious manner he received them all.

"Yes, yes, Monsieur Bédard, I know you very well. And you, Monsieur Picard. And you, Monsieur Plamondon. What a pleasure! Too young to remember? Not at all. I was already eighteen years old when I left St. Placide, now eight years ago. There, Madame Pouliot, you have my age exactly, but I am not sensitive on that point. Old enough to be settling down, you think? Yes, I was thinking of that myself. And what of the little Delima whom I used to see at school? Married? I am sorry to hear it — desolated. Ah, Madame Poisson, is it you? Charmed, I am sure. Monsieur and Madame Gosselin, too. Remember you? Certainly. *Mon Dieu*, how everything comes back to me! Have I not seen you passing along to church and to market in your spring carts, or in carts without springs? But now you drive in covered carriages in great style. What grandeur! What magnificence! How glad I am to see that everybody prospers, thanks to the good God!

"As for me, I am doing passably well, Monsieur Lebel, much better than in those days. Did I really drive to Quebec in the cart of Elzéar Buchon? Yes, certainly, and I shall not forget that good butcher's boy. I was not rich at that time, no indeed. The little money left by my good father had all been spent, excepting a small sum in the bank at Quebec. Did I arrive in Nevada by means of freight cars ? Oh, no, Monsieur Trembly, I was not reduced to that. After Quebec all was easy. Expensive living out there, Madame Trembly ? Well, you might think so. Bread, twenty cents the loaf; butter, fifty cents the pound; eggs, a dollar the dozen, and so on. If you could get such prices at Beauport you would soon be rich, would you not ? But you are already rich enough, as I see. In my days the ladies did not wear those fashionable hats, those French shoes, nor those fine cloaks trimmed with lace and braid, so *chic*, so becoming. Creations of Paris, are they not, Madame ?

"Is there gold in Nevada ? Yes, Joseph, my friend, plenty of it, if you know where to find it. Does everybody become rich out there ? No, I will not say that, but it is a good place for young men, if they have good health and some intelligence, if they work hard, if they do not drink nor gamble, nor keep loose company, nor steal horses, nor jump claims, nor look for trouble in any other way. Yes, Joseph, it is a good place for those who have luck, for those who survive.

"It would be a fine place for that son of yours, Madame Barbeau, that Napoléon with whom I used to play. What ? Here ? Is this my little Napoléon ? *Mon Dieu*, how you have grown ! What changes come while one is away ! You must be twenty-four at the very least. Still with papa and mama ? All the rest gone away ? Well, somebody must stay behind to take care of the farm, the cows, the pigs. It is amusing, feeding pigs. What appetites they have, what sweet voices, what gratitude ! And how they love to be scratched ! Ha ! Ha ! The pleasures of country life ! Nothing like that in Nevada.

"You would return with me, Napoléon ? Well, old man, that will not be hard to arrange. I am going back, of course, yet since yesterday I have had other thoughts. I have allowed myself to dream. Yes, Madame, I am still unmarried, an old bachelor, almost. There, the cat is out of the bag. The young ladies of Nevada do not suit me exactly. They have their merits, no doubt, but as to the figure, as to the complexion, as to the temper, as to the accomplishments of the housekeeper, they are not in the same class, I will say, with the young ladies of Quebec, of Beauport, of St. Placide. But tell me, Napoléon, who is that fine-looking man over there in the carriage, he with the grey hair ? Monsieur Taché ? Ah, I thought so. And that glorious blonde ? Mademoiselle Gabrielle ? Gabrielle ? I do not seem to remember. Ah, I have it. The little friend of Jean Baptiste. There, the events unfold, the secrets are revealed. It is fate, without a doubt. Napoléon, old man, present me. *Au revoir*, Monsieur, Madame, my friends."

"Monsieur Taché," said Napoléon Barbeau, as he and Pamphile, hat in hand, approached the carriage ; "Monsieur and Mademoiselle, I have the honour to present to you an old schoolfellow, Monsieur Pamphile Lareau, of Elko, Nevada."

"Much pleased, I am sure," said Monsieur Taché. "I remember you, I think, on account of some boyish prank of former days. But what of that ? The follies of that age are gone. Come to see us, Monsieur Lareau, during the week."

"I will come to-morrow, Monsieur Taché, with your permission and that of Mademoiselle."

Monsieur Taché smiled. "To-morrow if you wish,

Monsieur the stranger. We shall be glad to see you. *Au revoir*, Monsieur."

A little later, as Pamphile drove past the Giroux place, he saw Jean Baptiste in the yard unharnessing his horse.

"*Holà*, Jean Baptiste! *Holà*, little priest!" he called, in a tone of elation.

Jean raised his hat and smiled as the buggy drove by. In that smile Bonhomme and Madame Gagnon observed only the friendly greeting of a good neighbour; Mère Tabeau perceived the good-humoured toleration of a superior being; but Pamphile saw the confidence of a declared enemy and the menace of a threat half-revealed.

"It is chilly at present," he murmured. "The sun has gone behind a cloud. Or was it the manner of Jean Baptiste—a little frigid, perhaps?"

"Did you think so?" said Bonhomme Gagnon. "It was a very friendly salutation, I thought. Strange that we did not see him at the church."

"He was there," said Pamphile. "I saw him approaching the carriage of Monsieur Taché as Napoléon and I came up, but immediately he turned away."

"We were all looking at you, Monsieur," said Bonhomme Gagnon. "Jean Baptiste is with us all the time, as you know. Yet he also is a fine young man. Some say that he is much interested in Mademoiselle Taché; others say that it is Mademoiselle Laroche whom he favours. Who knows? He confides in nobody. But take care that you do not get in his way, Monsieur Lareau. It would be too dangerous. He is fierce, at times, they say, and strong as a bear."

"Let him keep out of my way, then," said Pamphile,

with a snarl, "for I am not accustomed to step aside for any man. I have lived too long in the West for that. I, too, might be dangerous, my good friend."

Bonhomme Gagnon made no reply, but surreptitiously crossed himself and muttered a prayer for protection against murder and sudden death.

CHAPTER XV

THE PASTIME OF LOVE

GABRIELLE was much offended at the behaviour of Jean Baptiste, not because he had refused to make the sacrifice which she had demanded, but because he had taken her at her word and had not insisted that she change her mind. If he had given up his great enterprise at her bidding she would have loved him less, or not at all. The knight who shunned the battle because of his lady's tears could never receive the prize of love. But after the battle, or during the intermissions of the conflict, he might at least come to see whether she could not smile through her tears. It was not necessary to choose between love and war when a brave man might have both for the asking.

Gabrielle wondered whether all men were as obstinate and as stupid as Jean Baptiste. For his stupidity she could pity him; for his obstinacy she could love him—almost. What an absurd person he was—how foolish, how blind! Who else would have chosen the hot, dusty road, when he might have taken the quiet, woodland path, a lover's walk, by her side? Since that afternoon he had been busy, so busy that he had found no time for friendship, no time for love, while the summer was slipping away and the golden days passing, never to return. When the day of love was gone, Jean would regret that he had trampled underfoot the precious jewels of the heart, the true values of life, in his blind pursuit of wealth and worldly success, vanities that could not satisfy the soul.

Besides, the success for which he was working might never come. Jean was a visionary person, a dreamer, a builder of cloud-castles. Presently they would fade away, those golden fancies, leaving nothing but a colourless, empty world, a desert, an aching desolation. Then, in the cold night of adversity, he would seek for love, but should not find it; he would ask, but should not receive; he would knock, but no door would be opened. Yes, he should be well punished for all his sins, and should spend many days in purgatory, without benefit of indulgence or intercession. After a time, perhaps, there would be forgiveness and reconciliation, but not until the whole debt, principal and interest, had been paid in full.

So Jean was going to fail. Who had said so? How could that be? Consider that tall, powerful frame, those broad shoulders, the massive head, the determined mouth and chin, the piercing eyes, the air of confidence and cheerful assurance that carried all before him. No, it was not in Jean Baptiste to fail. That which he began he would carry through to the end, in spite of everything. Every obstacle he would overcome; every enemy he would trample upon; every hindrance he would cast aside—yes, even the loving arms that would embrace him, the tender heart that would be his alone. And after all, when success had arrived, with riches, honour, power, and the crown of noble achievement, he would throw it all at the feet of another—at the feet of Blanchette Laroche.

And why Blanchette? Because she was not proud; because she did not ask much, and would be satisfied with little. He had only to call, to beckon, and she would follow him like a lamb—yes, like a poodle dog. So there was a way—the way of humility. That was what Jean demanded—submission, the surrender of the will, the abasement of the spirit. It was too much. Never should he have that—never!

On the contrary, it was Jean who should make the surrender. There was a man capable of a great passion, a passion not yet awakened, slumbering in the depths of his soul. For him love was a gentle emotion which he could subdue and forget at any time, a pastime which was never allowed to interfere with the more serious affairs of life. But what would he be when stirred to the depths of his being by a tempest of love? What would he do when the master passion was aroused and assumed control? Forget himself? Surely. Forget his plans, his ambitions, his cruel pride. Yes, he would forget all but love, and be willing to sacrifice all for love. And demand all? That also. And if he gave all and demanded all, who could resist, who could refuse? Not Gabrielle Taché. Would she go with this man to the end of the world? Yes, to the end of the world.

"Gabrielle, Gabrielle! Where are you, *Mignonne?* Where are you, Gabrielle?"

"Here, Mama," answered Gabrielle from the corner of the garden where she was sitting in the shade of an old apple-tree.

"Oh, there you are, day-dreaming, no doubt, while I have been looking for you high and low. And where are those flowers that you were to cut for the table an hour ago—yes, two hours? What have you been doing all this time? A fine wife you will make for an honest habitant. Eh, *Mignonne?*"

"No honest habitant for me," said Gabrielle, laughing gaily. "I should much prefer one of those brave officers of the Garrison."

"For shame, Gabrielle! A red-coat and a heretic."

"A red-coat, yes. I love red-coats, so bright, so gay. A heretic? Not at all. A good Catholic from the Highlands of Scotland, a brave, handsome soldier."

"Gabrielle, do not think of him. He is not for you. Presently his regiment will be transferred and he will go away to make new conquests. Oh, I know them of old, those gay soldiers. They come, they conquer, and they march away, leaving broken hearts. Do not think of him, Gabrielle."

"One must think of something, Mama. Who shall it be? Hormidas Vincent, perhaps? Or Isidore Bouchette? On the whole, I prefer Isidore—he has such glossy hair, so neatly parted in the middle, such adorable curls and such funny little silver rings in his ears. He has travelled, that one, in many parishes. I love peddlers—they have so many curious tales to tell, and so many that they do not tell. Such an air of mystery——"

"Gabrielle, be still. For mercy's sake stop your chatter. Do you know who is coming up the road?"

"Who, Mama, who? A young man? Isidore? What bliss!"

"Be tranquil, my dear, it is not Isidore."

"Who then? I am dying to know."

"It is monsieur the millionaire of Nevada."

"That snake!"

"Gabrielle, you are dreadful. Do not talk like that. It is a fine young man of an interesting type. His dress and manners are a little unusual, perhaps, but he is tall and handsome, with an air of melancholy quite engaging —like an artist or poet, I should say. And he is rich. Yes, a distinguished-looking young man, a personage. See, there he comes. Do not be rude to him, Gabrielle."

Gabrielle had no thought of being rude to Pamphile. On the contrary, she did her best to amuse him while her mother was preparing the dinner and her father was still in the hayfield. They played croquet on the lawn, walked about in the garden, sat on the green bench of the verandah looking out on the river and the mountains, and all the while they talked of this and that, of the scenery, the parish, the neighbours, the tourists, of Beauport, Quebec and Montreal, of Chicago and the Far West, of Nevada and the gold mines, of travel and adventure, of politics even, and religion. Pamphile was nothing if not interesting, for he had travelled much with his eyes open, was by nature of a ready wit and tongue, and knew how to tell of what he had seen and had not seen with a realistic abandon that was well-nigh irresistible.

At first Gabrielle could hardly conceal her aversion for Pamphile, who was, she felt, some evil genius of the underworld; but presently she forgot his outlandish dress, his gaudy jewellery, his long hair and his unctuous suavity, and saw only the tall, handsome, mysterious stranger who had descended upon the secluded valley from the great, unknown world beyond the mountains: It was a pleasure to hear him talk in an intimate way of people and things, to watch his animated gestures and changing expression, to wonder what had brought him to St. Placide and how long he would be able to stay.

Pamphile was a born story-teller, and, like most of

his tribe, his talk was chiefly of himself. He was the centre of every incident, the hero of every adventure. He spoke of the river and the great lakes, of mighty cities, of distinguished men, of the buffalo of the plains, of Indians and bandits, of lofty mountains and precipitous cañons, of cattle ranches and mining camps, of gamblers and shooting affrays; and always it was Pamphile who had been wise and generous, strong and brave, who had encountered all dangers, overcome all difficulties, and who had arrived at last at the summit of his ambition and was now enjoying a well-earned rest in the peaceful valley before plunging once more into the tumult and struggle of the outer world.

Gabrielle listened as one entranced, gazing in wonder at the mobile yet inscrutable face of Pamphile. Here certainly was a new type of man, such as she had not seen in St. Placide nor in Quebec, and certainly not within the walls of the Ursulines. She tried to imagine him in the garb of a priest, reading his breviary, hearing confession, giving consolation. Absurd! And how would he look in the uniform of the Garrison Artillery? Very funny, to be sure. He would certainly need to have his hair cut. What a pity he had not lived in the time of the Grand Monarch as an officer in a regiment of cavaliers—the Carignan Regiment, for example? There he would have been almost at home. But what a figure he would cut in the costume of a habitant! Ridiculous! No, Pamphile was a citizen of another world. In the West he was doubtless a great man, not at all out of place, and it was not fair to judge him by the standards of St. Placide. Why demand that he be exactly like other people? He was different. Not bad, only different.

"Gabrielle," said Madame Taché, after Pamphile had gone away, "you were right in your opinion of that man, after all. He is a species of serpent, as you said."

"Why, Mama!" exclaimed Gabrielle. "He is a fine young man, of an interesting type. His dress and manners are a little unusual, perhaps, but he is tall and handsome, with an air——"

"Be silent, Gabrielle. I have changed my mind since I have been able to observe him more closely. It is not his clothes, altogether, nor even his hair, nor that drooping moustache, but a certain expression of I know not what, an indefinable suggestion of evil. How glad I am that he has gone!"

"But, Mama, you were quite polite to him, and Papa, too, seemed to find him interesting."

"Naturally, one is polite to a guest. And he is interesting, far too interesting. He is fascinating, almost, like a serpent. Your father, of course, was glad to hear about the mines of Nevada. I hope he will not send any money there. No, Gabrielle, that man is not to be trusted, and I will not have him come again."

"But, Mama, he is to come to play a game of croquet to-morrow afternoon."

"Gabrielle, did you invite him?"

"No, Mama. Yes. That is, he asked if he might come; and I, what could I say?"

"That is a pity, my daughter. You should have spoken to me. What shall we do? We do not want to offend him. There, I have it. You shall go down to Quebec in the morning, and we will send a message of explanation to Monsieur Lareau. Mother Sainte Anne will be glad to see you."

"Oh, Mama, not that!" cried Gabrielle, with tears in her eyes. "Do not make me leave St. Placide just now, the lovely hills, the green fields, the leafy trees, the cool air. This is not the time to go to the city, so hot, so dusty. That little dark cell will be like a furnace, a veritable purgatory. No, Mama, you do not mean it. Do not send me away. It would be too cruel."

"Gabrielle, I am surprised at you. Usually you are glad to run down to Quebec for a few days, and Mother Sainte Anne is always kind. Nonsense, my dear child; you are too silly. You shall go, of course, and in a few days, possibly, you may return. We shall see."

"Well," said Gabrielle, with a sigh of resignation, "I will go, if you wish. You know best, Mama. As for that man from the West, he is nothing to me. Do you think that I should run away with him? Oh, it is to laugh. But he amuses me with his talk, I confess, like the quack-doctor whom we saw at the fair in Quebec. Could you not let me stay another day, one little day? One little afternoon's amusement, one little game of croquet—what is that? We must not offend people without reason, as you have said, even a man from the wild and woolly West. Say yes, Mama."

"Yes, yes, Gabrielle, if you will only stop your chatter. You make a person deaf. But remember—only one day, and you are not to see that young man after to-morrow. Do not say when you will return. That will remain undecided for the present."

"Mama, you are lovely. You are a saint, an angel, a bird of paradise. And I, too, am a species of bird, but very tame, I assure you. Do not worry about me. I will not fly away, but only flutter about for a few hours, and then hop meekly into the cage. It is a nice cage, and Mother Sainte Anne is a dear soul. I have often thought that I could be happy in that holy place for the rest of my life. Those who leave the world, and give themselves, body and soul, to the good God, find rest and peace on the bosom of infinite love, and the devotion which they give is returned to them a thousand-fold. Those are the words of Mother Sainte Anne herself. Oh, Mama, do not cry. You are not going to lose me. I have my moments of devotion, but they do not last long. I am too fond of you, of all my dear friends, of this brave world, and the glories of the religious life seem dim and far away. No, I have no vocation. There, dear, console yourself. Good-night. Sleep well."

It is a pleasant game, croquet, not only because it affords moderate exercise and demands a sufficient degree of skill, but also because it permits of frequent pauses, when the players may converse about the condition of the lawn, the position of balls and wickets, the ethics of various plays, the state of the weather, and what not, while they walk about on the soft grass, or rest, it may be, on rustic benches in the shade of trees. It is a game for lovers in the springtime of life, where there is no rivalry and where both may win. But when a third party comes there is a sudden change, the spirit of rivalry enters, and the innocent game becomes a form of war, a phase of the age-long struggle of life and death.

"Ah!" exclaimed Gabrielle, as Pamphile made a long hit, "that was a fine stroke. You play well, Monsieur Lareau, better than any one in our parish; that is, better than all but one."

"But one, you say, Mademoiselle Taché?" said

Pamphile, affecting an air of indifference. "And who is that, if I may dare to ask?"

"Oh," said Gabrielle, wishing to recall her words, "perhaps I am mistaken, for it is a long time since I have seen him play, but I was thinking of our neighbour, Monsieur Giroux."

"He?" said Pamphile, with a sneer. "The youth who was to have been a priest? Yes, I remember him. He must be a man by this time. Strange that he is still here among the stay-at-homes. Did he not dare to venture out into the world, where he might meet with men?"

"Monsieur Lareau," said Gabrielle, seriously, "it is evident that you do not know Monsieur Giroux, or you would not speak thus. He is very brave and very determined, and it is for that reason that he will not leave St. Placide."

"Oh, I can well understand, Mademoiselle," said Pamphile, with a knowing smile. "While there are such attractions here it is no wonder that he cannot tear himself away. For me, I also should like to stay in St. Placide. Tell me to stay, Mademoiselle."

Gabrielle blushed furiously.

"Monsieur Lareau, you take liberties. As for Monsieur Giroux, I know nothing of his affairs, but it is said that he has plans for the improvement of the parish, for the exploitation of the forest, the water-power and all that."

"Plans?" drawled Pamphile. "Designs? Intentions? Well, I also have plans, and I hope that the former candidate for holy orders will not interfere with them. So he plays croquet, it seems. A noble game, truly! I hope that he excels in other games demanding not less of skill, but more of intellect, of courage."

"He does," replied Gabrielle, now enlisted in defence of the local hero, "he knows how to play tennis, too, better than any of the tourists; and draughts and chess, like a master. He throws the hammer—oh, an enormous distance—and he can run like a deer, and leap like—like—a grasshopper."

"A grasshopper! Name of an insect! Ha! Ha! That is good. What a marvel, that priest that was to be! The sum of all the talents! But permit me to ask, Mademoiselle the defender, if the excellent youth knows how to shoot with the revolver, or with the rifle."

Gabrielle hesitated.

"Why do you ask, Monsieur Lareau?"

"Because," said Pamphile, between his teeth, "in the Far West that is the first thing that one thinks of, and the last."

Gabrielle grew pale.

"Monsieur Lareau," she begged, "please forget what I have said. I did not mean to offend you. Monsieur Giroux is nothing to me, but when you speak contemptuously of one of the neighbours, I wish, naturally, to defend him as much as possible. So please forgive me, Monsieur. It was discourteous in me, I know."

"Say no more, Mademoiselle Taché; it is I who have offended. I was perceiving a rival, that was all. If Jean Baptiste is not that he is my dear old schoolfellow, of whom I have often thought during my long years of exile. I should like to meet him again, for the sake of old times."

"That could be arranged," said Gabrielle, with

animation. "But no, alas, I shall not be here, for I am going away to-morrow, to Quebec."

Pamphile was aghast.

"To-morrow! And I had promised myself the pleasure of another game of croquet. Not to-morrow, Mademoiselle—the day after to-morrow, let us say."

"It is not I who decides these affairs, Monsieur, but my mother; and she is inflexible."

"Ah, cruel parent! Yes, I see, I see. Because I am not an eligible *parti*. Cruel parent! But surely Mademoiselle will return."

"Oh, yes, certainly. St. Placide is my home to which I return frequently. Before the end of the summer, no doubt."

"The end of the summer! Alas, long before that time I shall be on my way to Nevada, never to return. But will Mademoiselle be so kind as to tell me where she will be staying at Quebec?"

"Certainly, Monsieur," said Gabrielle, pathetically. "At the Convent of the Ursulines."

"A convent! *Mon Dieu!* Not to take the veil, I hope."

"Oh no," laughed Gabrielle, "not that, although I have sometimes thought of it. No, only to stay a while to receive a little more instruction in music, painting, embroidery, and all that. To finish, to be finished, you know."

"Yes, I know," sighed Pamphile. "It is I who am finished. But such is life. Mademoiselle Taché, you cannot imagine what a pleasure it has been——"

"Yes, and for me also," said Gabrielle, with a sad little smile. "It is such a pleasure to meet strangers, people who are different, you know. No, I shall not forget you. But there is Mama calling me. I must go. Good-bye, Monsieur Lareau. Good luck."

"But Mademoiselle, I have something else to say."

"I cannot wait, Monsieur. Some one is coming."

"Mademoiselle, it is of great importance, a matter of life and death, concerning our friend Monsieur Giroux, something which I must tell to you, and you alone. Well, if you will not, it is all the same to me. Adieu, Mademoiselle. Much pleased, I am sure."

"But, Monsieur Lareau, can you not write?"

"Absolutely impossible. To-morrow morning at sunrise I shall be back there in the forest where the path crosses the little stream, and I shall wait ten minutes."

"Monsieur, this is too much. I have the honour to bid you good evening."

"Good evening, Mademoiselle, and many thanks for all your kindness. And I shall be there at the time appointed."

On the following morning, as the sun rose above the hill, peeping through the thick foliage he perceived Pamphile Lareau reclining upon a mossy bank beside the little brook that flowed through a shady glen to join the main river about half a league below. His broad-brimmed hat lay on the ground beside him, his long black mane fell on his neck and shoulders, and he was twisting the ends of his moustache as he smiled expectantly—a smile that was not good to see. In the clear morning light there was no illusion of romance or chivalry about Pamphile. The glamour of the evening twilight was gone, and he appeared as he was, a beast of prey, a panther ready to spring upon the passer-by.

Suddenly he became aware of a presence, and glancing

up he saw Gabrielle, pale and beautiful as the morning, looking at him with awakened and startled eyes. He saw no change in her, but smiled exultantly as he slowly rose and held out his arms.

"A fine morning, Gabrielle."

Gabrielle drew back.

"You presume, Monsieur Lareau," she said, coldly. "You presume upon a too slight acquaintance. But no matter. Will you have the kindness to give me your message?"

"Oh, time enough for that. The day is young. Let us talk a little. Let us look at the trees, listen to the birds, watch the clear stream as it flows along. Let us enjoy the beauty of the morning, the charm and seclusion of the woods. No? What?"

"I have no time for that," said Gabrielle, impatiently flicking her boot with the riding-whip which she carried in her hand. "If you please, Monsieur Lareau, give me the message."

"Message? There is no message," said Pamphile, with a leer. "That was understood, was it not? It was only to say good-bye."

"No message?"

"No. That is to say, yes. A moment, Mademoiselle. Come back, for the love of God. It is here, the message, the letter. Allow me to hand it to you. It will explain everything. There, I have you, little bird. Do not wriggle so. A kiss. One only. No? Then I take it—thus and thus. Ah! *Sacrée diable de femme! Sacré!*"

Pamphile's note of triumph ended in a scream of rage and pain, for Gabrielle, wrenching herself free from his grasp, turned on him with flaming face and blazing eyes, and with the raw hide whip struck him twice across the face. Immediately she fled up the path, calling loudly for help.

"Jean! Jean! To me! To me! Ah, *Mon Dieu!* Jean! Jean!"

With sublime faith in the hour of danger Gabrielle was demanding a miracle; and lo! her cry was answered, for it was Jean himself who came running down the path in time to catch her in his arms as she was on the point of falling to the ground.

"Gabrielle, what is it? What is the matter, dear? Ah, I see. The whip—give it to me. So it is you—thief, dog! Stand there! A fine face you have. There, take that—and that! Shoot, would you? Drop it! Good. Take two more! There! And there! It is a wonder I do not kill you. Go!"

Pamphile slunk away like a whipped cur, but with murder in his heart. Jean watched him until he disappeared in the forest, and then turned slowly, as one in pain.

"Gabrielle!"

But Gabrielle was gone.

CHAPTER XVI

THE TEMPTATION OF JEAN BAPTISTE

"Jean! Jean! To me! To me!"

The cry seemed but an echo in the recesses of the woods, yet Jean could not rid himself of the feeling that Gabrielle was still in danger and in need of help. The same vague sense of danger had come to him a little while before, as he stood on the doorstep of his house, smoking his pipe, watching the sunrise, and planning the day's work, and had brought him running along the road to the Taché place and thence down the woodland path to meet her whom he loved best and him whom he most hated. They had met; the danger was past; and now it seemed to Jean that he was totally indifferent to Pamphile and that he hated Gabrielle more than any other being in all the world. Answer her cry for help? Never again!"

"Jean! Jean!"

The call was fainter now, with a note of reproach and the suggestion of a sob, but Jean gave no heed. He only stood there, his heart full of jealousy and anger, thinking evil thoughts. A strange meeting, surely, on that lonely path at such an hour. A coincidence? Hardly. Pre-arranged? Doubtless. To what end? Who can understand the heart of a woman? To meet a stranger by accident on a Sunday morning, after Mass, to have one visit and another, a game of croquet, and then———. Love at first sight, it would seem, and after that a rapid career, a swift descent into the depths. Inconceivable? Yes. Impossible? Nothing is impossible. Even the holy angels could fall from Heaven, and the Son of God might have bowed down to Satan.

But the whip? Jean held it up in his clenched hand, a short but heavy raw-hide with a knotted tail and loaded head, a dangerous weapon in strong and determined hands. She had come alone, but not unprotected. And those marks on the face of Pamphile? Inflicted by the selfsame whip, evidently. By whose hand? The hand of Gabrielle. Jean's heart gave a leap at the thought, and he almost smiled. She had struck Pamphile twice with the knotted tail, and if Jean had not come to the rescue she would have turned at bay and felled her assailant to the ground with the leaden head. Brave Gabrielle! A girl of spirit, that, a girl worthy of any man.

How then could she be ensnared by that spider, be fascinated by that serpent? But she had broken the spider's net; she had escaped the wiles of the serpent. A lover's quarrel? Only lovers quarrel; the indifferent never. But do they strike each other with a whip? No, thank God, Gabrielle did not love Pamphile. Impossible. As for the rest, what matter? Strange, certainly, that meeting in the woods, but not more strange than his own arrival in the nick of time. The world itself is strange, and the combinations, the possibilities, infinite. All is strange, mysterious, improbable. Nothing can be explained. One must have faith in one's friends, in oneself, in God. No; she cared nothing for that reptile. A passing fancy, perhaps, but even that was over—else why the blow, the flight, the cry for help? On whom does one call in the hour of danger? On one's friends, first of all, and then, in the last extremity, on God.

"Jean! Jean!"

A low voice seemed to call to him from the hill, a voice as of one in tears.

Jean awoke from his reverie, and ran up the path.

"Gabrielle!" he called. "I am coming, dear. No danger. I am here. Gabrielle! Gabrielle! where are you?"

The voice of Jean awoke the echoes of the hills, but there was no other reply. On he ran with fear in his heart, peering into the woods on either side, and calling incessantly, until he reached the place where the path left the forest, and he could see the home of Gabrielle nestling in a hollow in the midst of green fields, with its white walls, its spacious verandah, its black roof with dormer windows, and its massive stone chimney from which a wisp of yellow smoke rose in the morning air. It was a picture of comfort and security; and, as Jean looked upon the peaceful scene, he assured himself that his fears were groundless and that all was well.

There was, however, a slight commotion about the place, such as one might expect to see on a market day or on the departure of some member of the family for a visit to the city. A large valise lay on the verandah, and at intervals Madame Taché or a maid appeared with a parcel or two, a parasol, a cloak, a basket. Monsieur Taché and one of the men hurried to the barn; presently the great doors were flung open and a prancing pair of bays came out with a carriage, as though the family were going to Mass, to a wedding, or some other notable celebration. Jean could hear the wheels crunch on the gravel as they drove around to the front steps, where the valise and the parcels were put on in front with the driver, while Madame Taché and Gabrielle came out of the house all ready to depart.

It was Gabrielle herself, dressed all in white, like a bride, a white cloak on her shoulders and a white hat with a single white plume above her golden hair. Jean could not see her face in the distance, but she seemed loth to go, for she ran hither and thither saying good-bye to everybody, even to the chickens and geese, patted Boule, the dog, on the head with a lingering caress, and then threw her arms about her father's neck, sobbing bitterly.

Jean turned away with tears in his eyes, and when he looked again the bays were prancing along the road, strong and proud, as though carrying a queen and a princess to a wedding feast. Never was princess more beautiful and more sad, for she had the air of one who was forsaking all that she held most dear, and going away never to return. As she passed near the place where Jean was standing she looked up once with an appealing glance, but made no sign of recognition or farewell. It was as if she did not see him, but was looking beyond into the depths of the woods. As the carriage came to the turn of the road Gabrielle turned and waved her handkerchief toward her old home. Perhaps Jean was included in the farewell. At any rate, he waved back, and as the carriage disappeared from sight he thought he caught a flutter of white meant for him alone.

Jean took a long breath, and then another, to keep down the tide of emotion that was surging up from the depths of his soul. Then, pulling himself together with a mighty effort, he sprang over the fence and strode down the road toward his own home at a terrific pace, as though to escape as fast as possible from the place where he had seen the vanishing of all his hopes. For Jean did not deceive himself; he understood it all; could see it all, as in a vision. Gabrielle, that angel in the white robes, was leaving St. Placide—for ever. She was going to a wedding—her own—in the chapel of the Ursulines, before a congregation of black-robed sisters. She would be a bride—the bride of Christ. They would cut off her golden hair, dress her in black from head to foot, and make her say infinite prayers by night and day on the cold, stone floor. Did Christ demand that?

"I do not believe that He will have that," said Jean, aloud. "But if so, I protest. It is not just. By Heaven, it is not! Ah, why did I not answer at the first call? Why did I not follow? Fool that I was! Yes, fool, fool!"

"Not so fast, Jean Baptiste," said a voice directly in front of him. "Stop! You are running me down! Stop, I say! There you have done it! *Sacré diable!* Fool! Yes, fool, fool!"

Jean stopped at last in his mad career, looked about in a dazed manner, and saw a little old man picking himself up from the dusty road, while filling the air with curses.

"Why, Monsieur Laroche, is it you? What is the matter? You fell down? I ran over you? Surely not. *Mon Dieu*, Monsieur, if I did I am sorry. Forgive me, I beg of you. It was an accident, I assure you. I was not thinking; that is to say, I was thinking of something else. There, Monsieur, allow me to brush off the dust, and to hand you your hat. Oh, but I am sorry. What can I say?"

"Nothing!" said the old man, with a vicious snap of the jaws. "Say nothing! Don't speak to me! I will get even with you. Yes, I will punish you for this, Monsieur the Proprietor, Monseigneur the Millionaire that is to be. Yes, I will show you."

"Well, Monsieur Laroche, if you feel like that I can do no more. Good-day, Monsieur."

"Not so fast, Jean Baptiste Giroux," said the old man, with malicious deliberation. "Not so fast, my enterprising friend. Remember, if you please, the little payment that is coming to me, the half-yearly interest that will be due next week."

"Well, what of it?" said Jean.

"You will pay it," said the money-lender, with a leer, "on the very day."

"Of course," said Jean, with contempt. "Is that all you wished to say?"

"Yes. No," said the old man, taken by surprise, for he had expected Jean to ask for an extension. "You will pay it when due—on the very day? Well, I like that. It pleases me. It is not often that one finds a young man of such a talent for affairs, of such promptitude. It is a good sign, Jean Baptiste. You will succeed, no doubt, if you have good luck. Yes, a promising young man. If only I had a partner like you, a son-in-law. What? It could be arranged, could it not? The little daughter has refused, of course, but might change her mind. Who can tell? Women are variable, as you know. What do you say, Jean, my lad—shall we have a try?"

"Monsieur Laroche," said Jean, earnestly, "I have

the greatest respect for Mademoiselle Blanchette, and I would not for the world have you persuade her to change her mind. These marriages of convenience are generally unsuitable and often terrible. It is a dreadful thing—marriage without love."

Bonhomme Laroche laughed aloud.

"Jean Baptiste Giroux, you talk like a fool. Marriage of convenience ? And why not ? The union of two good farms, with buildings, implements, cattle, horses, and all that, appears to me very convenient and suitable. Moreover, on one side a fine hotel, on the other an ample dowry — what better could you desire ? Marriage without love ? It is to laugh. Go home, Jean ; regard yourself in the glass, and consider. Six feet in your stockings, straight as a tamarack, broad shouldered, strong as an ox, a great chief, a leader of men. What girl could not love a man like you ? They have eyes, those creatures, you may believe. And my Blanchette—what beauty, what good temper, what capacity ! Jean, my lad, it is all right ; it will go, it is a match made, I will say, in Heaven. Yes, say nothing ; it is to be."

Jean was speechless, for the little old man, pouring forth a torrent of words, fairly danced with excitement and finally flung his arms about the young man's neck in token of complete reconciliation.

"Jean, Jean, my son. It will arrange itself. Say nothing. I will not hear. Go. That little payment— forget about it. What is that among friends ; yes, relations. There, not a word. All is forgotten. Go home, I say, for the present. Adieu ! Adieu !"

It was still early in the morning, for Jean had been away from home scarcely an hour—an hour that seemed an immeasurable time, during which he had seen his past life unroll before him like a writing in a foreign language, dark and meaningless. During that time he had seen his ideals, his plans, his dream-castles melt away into nothing, and all his future become a blank. The sun was still shining, the clouds still floating in the sky, the grass still green, the birds still singing, the air still fragrant with the odours of pine and balsam, of crushed strawberries and new-mown hay—but not for him. The world to him seemed colourless, odourless, silent as the tomb, because the light and joy had gone out of his life when a young girl with blue eyes and golden hair had passed down the road clad all in white as a bride adorned for her husband. She had vanished at the turn of the road, and immediately the world was changed.

The glory of the world had departed; the beauty was gone; love had flown away; and life was no longer worth while. Even the great house, the work of his hands, his castle and seat of pride, was like a broken toy, a thing to be thrown aside. It had ceased to interest him, but still the force of habit led him thither. He pressed the latch, and entered the great kitchen where his good mother was preparing breakfast.

"Good morning, Jean," she said, looking up with a smile, which immediately changed to a look of alarm, "Oh, Jean, what is it? What is the matter? Where have you been? What is it, Jean, my son?"

"It is nothing, my mother," he said, with a fugitive smile. "Nothing at all. That is, I am a little tired, perhaps."

"Tired? A great man like you, and at this time of the day! Six o'clock on a fine summer morning—and tired! Very strange, that. No, Jean, you are putting me off. What is it, then? Tell me, my son."

"It is Bonhomme Laroche, my mother."

"That old miser. What does he want?"

"His money."

"His money? We have not had it six months, and the loan was for three years."

"It is the interest that he wants, my mother, the half-yearly interest."

"Well, that is not much, a matter of sixty dollars or so. We will pay him."

"Yes, we will pay him, of course, but we shall not have much left."

"Nonsense, Jean! We shall have still a nice little deposit in the bank; the tourists owe us a good sum; and to-morrow we shall send butter and eggs to the market—five dollars worth at the very least. No, there is no cause for worry. The business is going well. It will come out all right, with the help of the good God. Have courage, my son. The time of sowing will soon be over, and you will see the golden harvest, the fruit of all your planning, your work. If that is all—no?"

"He wishes to buy a husband for his daughter."

"For his daughter—for Blanchette? Yes, I know. All the rest are married—long ago. Only the little Blanchette is left. Not so very little now, nor so very young. Let us see — ten, twenty, twenty-five, yes, twenty-six years this summer. I remember well—fourteen years after we came to the parish. They were sufficiently poor then, those Laroches, poor and not at all proud. But they are not so very proud even now, although quite rich. And the little Blanchette was pretty, too, before the smallpox. A clever girl, and excellent housekeeper, a manager from the bottom, a worker, too. No, it is not a bad suggestion, not at all.

"Yes, she would be a fine partner for one who owns a hotel. No fear of failure after that. All anxiety gone, all concern for the future. The dowry would be considerable. She would have that fine farm, with cattle, horses, pigs, sheep, implements, furniture, linen, and all that, not to speak of money in the bank. Bonhomme Laroche has explained it to me many times. A strange man, that. A miser, true, but a just miser. He will have his money always, to the last *sou*, but no more. I hope that we may be able to pay him all, when due. There are great risks in an enterprise like this, and great responsibilities. The alliance would settle everything, remove all difficulties, dispel all clouds. Think of it, Jean. The two farms united— a veritable estate, a seigniory, almost. Ah, my son, if your father were alive, how pleased he would be!"

"My father," said Jean, thinking aloud, "would he have sold himself in this way, I wonder?"

"Your father, Jean, would be pleased to see your prosperity, as I have said, but for himself he did not regard such things. They had no power over him. He did not know the value of money, that man. For him truth, honour, a good name, were the true values, more precious than rubies, more desirable than all the gold of the world. And love? Yes, love above all. He also could have married an heiress, the daughter of a rich merchant, a ship-owner. Beautiful she was, I must confess, beautiful and accomplished. Yet he preferred me, me. I never knew why. Ah, *Mon Dieu*, what devotion! Did he ever regret it? He never said so. On the contrary, he assured me many times—— And I, did I regret the poverty, the work, the long years? No, it was my glory. And you, Jean, my son, are like him, and I know what you will do. Yes, and you are right, both of you. Land, cattle, money, are very fine, all right in their place, but in comparison with love they do not count for much. Ah, selfish old woman that I am to wish you to give up so much for the sake of a dowry. Jean, my son, you shall not, you could not."

"No, my mother, it would be impossible."

"Well, let us say no more about it. Let us think of something else. There are still good fish in the sea, although they are often hard to catch. That little Gabrielle, for example, the most beautiful girl, they say, in all the parishes. Even in Quebec, there is not her equal. They are rare, you know, blondes of that type, with hair like a sunset cloud, not red, not gold, but something of both, and changing with the light. And such a complexion, such a lovely face, and a smile that touches the heart. A sufficiently good temper, also, not meek, but high-spirited, polite and altogether charming. An ample dowry, too, which is not to be despised when all the rest is there. It contributes to independence and harmony.

"A most independent young lady, not easily caught, I should say, but a prize for any fisherman. I have heard of several young men who have aspirations—a brave young officer of the Artillery, for one. They are dangerous rivals, those young soldiers, with their fine clothes, their noble bearing, their self-confidence. I remember them well. They are irresistible, almost. And Gabrielle is no ordinary habitant girl, but one who would be at home in any society, high or low. She will fly away some day, I fear. I don't like to think of that, for the parish will be different without her. Yes, very different.

"But, Jean, what is the matter? Where are you going? Sit down again, please. Your breakfast is just ready. See, I have something that you like, a nice piece of ham, some eggs, and the most delicious pancakes."

"Thank you, dear," said Jean, wearily, "but I have no appetite this morning."

"No appetite? That is serious. What is wrong? Work to do? Nonsense! How can one work if one does not eat? Do not go, my son. At least, come back soon, soon. There, I have driven him away. Talkative old woman! Stupid old creature! My poor Jean!"

CHAPTER XVII

VENGEANCE

THE brief summers are warm in St. Placide—how else could the crops of hay, oats, and potatoes come to maturity?—but usually the nights are cool, that the habitants, who have toiled many hours in the hot sun, may enjoy refreshing sleep and be ready at the point of dawn for the work of another day. But now and then, in the dog days, there comes a blistering day, followed by a hot and sultry night, when tired people lie awake for hours, longing in vain for rest.

The night following the departure of Gabrielle was such a night as this, and Jean Baptiste, finding the heat of his attic insupportable, went out on the railed terrace that crowned the roof, and lay down under the stars. There was not a breath of air, and no sound to be heard but the steady murmur of the river in the valley below. The beasts that prowl by night made no noise; the bats flitted silently to and fro; now and then an owl passed like a shadow; here and there the lamp of a firefly glimmered and went out; and the stars twinkled wearily as though they would fain close their eyes in sleep.

Jean did not sleep, but lay thinking of his past life, his ambitions and struggles, his hopes and fears, his successes and failures, as though trying to strike a balance of profit and loss that should give value to his life or show how empty it was of all worth and meaning.

He had always assumed that life was worth living—but why ? In God's name, why ?

To know, to understand ? He had read much in printed books and in the book of nature ; he had tried to think, to guess, to imagine the answer to the riddle of existence, but with what result ? All was mystery, shrouded in darkness, silent, speechless, with only a twinkling light here and there to lead—or mislead. To know ? That could not be the end of life, for what could one know ? Nothing.

To love ? Ah, there was something to fill the heart with joy—and pain. When one finds a human being so beautiful that one would gaze on her for ever, so sympathetic that in her company one has an enduring sense of harmony and peace, so dear that one would fain be with her until the end of time and afterwards in the eternal world—when one finds such perfection of loveliness, surely it is the perfection of existence to love and to be loved. Yes, but if one were not loved. If in the early morning she went away, of her own free will, to be the bride of another, what could one do with that consuming love but tear it from the heart, that one might give oneself heart and soul to the work of life ?

The work of life ? There at last was something for the strong hand and brain, something to occupy the thought, to drive out the spirit of despair, to fill the life with action, to cause one to forget the mystery of existence and the shipwreck of love. To work, to build, to create, to find the expression of oneself in the work of one's hands, and, finally, like God, to pronounce it good—there was achievement to satisfy the soul. If only the works of man, like the works of God, could last for ever ! Yet even these would pass away. Out of the darkness of primeval chaos all had come ; back to chaos and darkness all would go. Yes, even the works of God. And God Himself ? What was He but the creator of a vain show, the spirit of deceit and futility ? It is written that He repented that He had made Man. What wonder ?

Jean Baptiste, as he lay there in the gloom of night, was wandering, in thought, away from the realities of daily life, far from the trodden paths, beyond all landmarks, into the confused and misty regions where no reason dwells, but doubt, madness, and fell despair, and where there is a downward path that plunges the lost soul into the abyss.

From these evil dreams he was awakened by the rumbling of thunder, and the falling of great drops of rain from a black cloud that passed, like a curtain, across the sky. Flashes of lightning lit up the valley, showing the trees of the forest bending before the wind, while here and there a broken trunk stood erect with naked limbs from which the branches had been torn by the fury of the gale. Presently the storm arrived, shaking the house to its foundations ; the rain came down in torrents ; and from the inky sky there fell lurid forks of lightning followed by crashing thunder, the sound of falling trees, and the cries of terrified beasts and men. It was a terrific, a sublime spectacle, a display of power before which the timid soul cowers and shrinks and seeks a place of refuge, a hole wherein to creep, if by any chance it may escape the vengeance of the awful power against which it cannot contend. Not so Jean Baptiste, who enjoyed the refreshing bath of rain and the brilliant display of colour, and to whom thunder claps were reassuring, since he knew that he who hears the thunder has not yet been touched by the lightning. But suddenly there appeared a great blaze of violet light, with a little crackling noise, and for Jean Baptiste the show was ended. The bolt of God had fallen upon La Folie, and the master of the house was very close to death.

Immediately after this, as it seemed to Jean—it was more than an hour—he felt himself roughly shaken, and heard a voice calling, as from a great distance.

"Wake up! Wake up, Jean! *Mon Dieu*, will he never hear? Wake up, I say. We must get down out of this."

"Get down?" said Jean, drowsily, without opening his eyes. "Get down? But no, it is comfortable here. Let me alone, please. I am sleepy, sleepy."

"There, you are all right, I see," said the voice, louder now. "But get up, quick, quick! Get up, or I will throw you down. *Sacré fou!* Take that!"

"Don't kick me," said Jean. Then, opening his eyes, he stared at his assailant.

"Oh, it is you, Pamphile, and you kick me? Well, I don't wonder. Do it again, my friend, and after that I will throw you off the roof. But how black your face is! And where is your hair? *Mon Dieu!* What has happened?"

"Happened? *Sacré bleu!* Your house is on fire. I tell you. Fire! Fire! Get up, you cursed idiot, and save yourself. For the last time—get up!"

As Jean rose to his feet black volumes of smoke were rolling up from the stairway, and he could hear the roar of flames below. He started down the stairs.

"Not there, you fool!" yelled Pamphile. "I passed

that way two minutes ago, and see me now. This way! We can slip down the roof on this side and then jump to the ground. Are you ready?"

"Yes," said Jean, slowly, "and I am sorry that I struck you with the whip. It would have been better——"

"Shut up!" said Pamphile, savagely. "You shall pay for that, oh yes. But at present we must save ourselves. *Dieu*, but it is hot! This way. The roof will hold, I think. Prepare to jump in a moment. No, that will not be necessary—they have placed a ladder. There is some intelligence left, I see. Steady, now. Slowly. No danger. There, you are on earth again. *Par Dieu!* It was a close shave. The roof has fallen in. Madame, I have the honour to present to you Monseigneur de la Folie, the biggest damn fool in St. Placide—yes, in all Canada."

"Listen to that," said one of the neighbours, who had hastened to the scene at the first alarm. "That is what I have always said. Jean Baptiste was a big fool to build a house like that—yes, a damn fool, as Monsieur the millionaire has said. It is a brave man, that millionaire. And Madame is glad to see her son again."

"Yes," said Bonhomme Gagnon, with an air of importance, "it was I, you see, who was the first to arrive. Already the house was in flames. The people were safe—that is to say, all but Jean, who sleeps in the attic. Madame was distracted, frantic. 'Where is Jean? Oh, where is Jean?' she screamed. 'Jean, my Jean! He will be burned to death.' She rushed to the door, going to run upstairs through all the smoke and flame. 'No, no, Madame,' I said, 'you cannot.

Wait a minute. Jean will waken, no doubt, in a moment. If not, I will go myself.' But she would not listen.

"Then comes along Monsieur Pamphile, his face white as a sheet, but all marked with red stripes as though some one had struck him with a lash. What was the cause of that, I wonder? 'Stop, Madame!' he cried. 'I will find the little priest. I will bring him down to you.' He did not go in by the door—that was impossible—but climbed up to one of the windows of the second floor, and went in. 'There is a good man gone to his death,' said I to myself. But presently he appeared on the roof, as you have seen. It was lucky I thought of the ladder, was it not? It was I who said: 'Bring the ladder.' You heard me, Damase."

"Yes," said Damase Gosselin, with a smile; "you were saving the life of a tourist, I think."

"Naturally," said Bonhomme Gagnon, with some asperity, "I was assisting everybody."

"And meanwhile," continued Damase, "the millionaire from Nevada ascends to the rescue of Jean Baptiste. It is a hero, that millionaire. But where is he? Disappeared, vanished! That is the way with heroes. They are modest people. One never hears them blow their own horn."

"That is true," said Bonhomme Gagnon, nodding his head vigorously. "The brave are always humble. That is the way with me, for example. I never like to talk of myself, for fear somebody will laugh at me. It is enough to have a good conscience, no matter what people think. But I will tell you, in confidence, that it was I who first saw the fire, who gave the alarm.

Without me no Pamphile, no Jean Baptiste descending by the ladder."

The neighbours crowded about Bonhomme Gagnon, who went on, impressively:—

"Yes, I heard the clap of thunder, of course. Who could sleep on such a night? 'There,' I said, 'something was struck. La Folie, perhaps, standing alone on the hill, with no lightning-rods.' I went to look, but could see nothing. At the next flash there was La Folie, the same as ever. It was only a tree, I thought. Soon the rain ceased, and I sat on the steps smoking my pipe, and looking at the clouds as they cleared away. I thought to myself: 'La Folie will get it sooner or later. The good God does not love a man like Jean Baptiste, so proud, so ambitious, so avaricious, one who would change everything, overturn everything—an atheist, almost. Yes, the good God will punish him some day.' It was prophetic, that thought of mine, for after a while I saw a bright light in one of the windows at La Folie, and then a great blaze that lit up the whole house. I made a jump, you may be sure, called Marie, François, Isidore, Suzette—all the family. 'Fire! Fire!' I called, and ran as fast as I could up the hill. *Dieu*, but it was an excitement."

"What a pity that you cannot run fast, Monsieur Gagnon!" said Damase. "If you had arrived sooner you might have saved Jean yourself."

"Very true," said Bonhomme Gagnon, "and I would have done it, you may be sure, but for those tourists. When I arrived they were descending from the windows, some in night-gowns, some with trousers on; and one, that Englishman over there, with all his clothes, an eye-glass even. 'Here, my man,' he said, 'if you will bring me a ladder I will step out of this, for it is deucéd hot.' I was carrying the ladder when Madame appeared wringing her hands, and then came Pamphile, as you know."

" The Englishman offered to pay you well, no doubt," suggested Damase.

" Yes. No. That is to say, he mentioned a certain sum, but I could not think of it. I was saving life, you see, human life, which is of more value than money. Afterwards, if he had felt that his life was worth five or ten dollars, I might have been persuaded—— But I could do nothing for him. Madame wanted the ladder for her son, who, naturally, seemed of great importance to her, and I placed it by the roof, just in time."

" Monsieur Gagnon," said Damase, emphatically, " you also are a hero, that is evident. What a pity that such heroes cannot receive a substantial reward— five dollars, at least, for every life that they save ! The life of that Englishman must be worth at least that amount. Let us ask him for it, Monsieur Gagnon."

" No, no!" spluttered Bonhomme Gagnon. " I would not for the world. He has lost his eye-glass, and is in a bad temper."

" True," said Damase, " and when you took the ladder away he was in a fine rage. It was a pleasure to see him. His bath-tub also was consumed, and his sponge. But the good God let him off easy compared with poor Jean. But tell us, Monsieur Gagnon, is it true Jean has said that the good God did not cause the fire? Is he really an atheist, as they say ? "

" Not so loud, Damase," whispered Bonhomme Gagnon. " He might hear you. See him over there as he watches his fine house burn to ashes. He is angry, as you may imagine. He has lost money—more than the farm is worth. Insurance? None at all. He was a fool, as Pamphile has said, one with too much confidence in himself and too little in the good God. An atheist? Very likely. Who else would want to build an hotel in St. Placide, to bring tourists to our peaceful parish, to introduce strange fashions, to corrupt the youth, to overturn everything? And he wishes to make a dam across the St. Ange, to build a factory, to create a city. Yes, he would change all the old ways, the good customs, the holy religion, even. An atheist? Very likely. But the good God was against him, as we have seen, and Jean Baptiste is finished. He will be a habitant, like the rest of us, or he will leave the parish. Well, let him go. We were here before he was born, and shall be all right after he is gone. St. Placide has no need of Jean Baptiste."

The mind of Bonhomme Gagnon had been poisoned against Jean by his association with Pamphile and Mère Tabeau, and the rest of the neighbours were strangely ready to think ill of him and to believe that he had been justly punished for his pride and presumption. He had wished to set himself upon an eminence far above the neighbours, and had tried to make himself a great lord, a species of pope, in the parish of St. Placide; but the good God, seeing that he held his head so high, had brought him down and humbled him in the dust. His great house was a heap of ashes; his plans were shattered, his prospects ruined; and he who had thought himself the perfection of all the virtues, the sum of all the talents, was finding by bitter experience that he was only a common man. Every man must learn this lesson, sooner or later, that his pride may be broken, his spirit chastened, that he may be able to bear the yoke, to walk side by side with his fellows and to walk humbly before his God. Thus the neighbours, by a strange mixture of piety and hypocrisy, conspired to humble one who had dared to raise his head above them, and deified the envy and malice of their own hearts.

Mère Tabeau was at the fire, to see and hear everything; but on this occasion, strange to say, she kept in the background, and had little to say beyond assenting, with nods and knowing looks, to all that was said in disparagement of Jean Baptiste. Before the fire was quite burned out, and before the neighbours had dispersed, she slipped away to her little hut, where she found Pamphile seated before a cracked mirror, carefully trimming, by the light of a candle, the remains of his once flowing mane of glossy black hair.

"Eh, my nephew," she cackled. "Eh, Monsieur the millionaire, Monsieur the hero, you have been singed a little, I see. What a pity!"

"Yes," drawled Pamphile, "it is a great loss to me. That *chevelure* was part of my capital, you see—useful in my business, you understand. It was part of the make-up, my dear aunt, like the white tie and the diamond. It was to me what the silk hat is to the advocate, the tonsure to the priest, the biretta to the cardinal, the tiara to the pope. I was in good company, my dear aunt, but now I am shorn of my strength, a common man."

"Nom de nom!" ejaculated Mère Tabeau. "You are a devil to talk like that at such a time. You will be joking when you are going to the gallows."

"Without doubt, my dear aunt. Life itself is a

joke; and death is the best joke of all. The only trouble is to see the point of it, whether it is man, God, or the devil who is fooled. For me, I think it is the devil who is the butt, and I laugh at him. Ha! Ha! Foolish old devil! We make him think that we belong to him, and in the end we die in the odour of sanctity. Ha! Ha! What a joke! You see it, my lovely aunt?"

"*Sacré!*" said Mère Tabeau. "*Sacré!*"

"If that is all you have to say I think that I will go to bed," drawled Pamphile, with a yawn.

"No, no, my nephew, let us talk a while. Such a night of adventure we have not had for many a year, not since the smugglers came across from Chateau, with the military after them. That was excitement, if you like. But this affair at La Folie was not so bad. You choose a good night for the fire, my nephew. What?"

Pamphile stared at the old hag.

"I?" he said. "I choose? But no, my wise aunt, it was the good God. That thunderbolt, you know."

"Bah!" she sneered. "It made a big noise, the thunder; knocked a few stones off the chimney, put Jean Baptiste to sleep, but that was all. No, my friend, the good God had nothing to do with it."

"But the fire——"

"Started an hour later, in the wood-pile near the stove."

"My dear aunt, you seem to be well informed."

"Informed? I was there and I saw. I am a light sleeper, you must know; and when you, my dear guest and nephew, left my house in the dead of night, I became curious, as any woman would, followed at a safe distance, and saw everything — saw you strike the match, even. I tell you, my western friend, that it is better to confide in people, especially one's near relations. Too much secrecy is bad for the health, leading to serious trouble, in which case one might have to call in the physician, that is to say, the police. Eh, my dear nephew?"

"Ah, my lovely aunt, you have the advantage of me, I must confess, in these days of enlightenment, of emancipation. If only the good old days could come again I would know what to do. I would have you drowned as a witch, or burned, perhaps. Yes, that would be better—a little taste of Hell in advance, a sample, as it were, of what is to follow. Eh, my angel aunt?"

"Pamphile," said the old witch, "you are a devil, and I love you for it. In the old days at Chateau there were lovers like you, brave boys, fearing neither God nor man. Usually man is more to be feared, but in the end God and the devil. But the devil amuses one for a time. If only I could be young again! But tell me, Pamphile, my friend—why did you not let him die?"

"Well, my aunt, that is a hard question. Why did I not let him be burned to a cinder? How do I know? I thought of it, to be sure; and I said to myself: 'There, Pamphile, you are avenged. Be satisfied.' But what revenge can one take on an enemy dead? No, it was better that Monseigneur should see his castle burn to the ground. A good revenge, my precious aunt. First you take away one's love, then one's property, then the ambition that makes life worth living; and after that, to finish, you give the *coup de grace*. That was one of my reasons, perhaps.

"For another, I hear Madame Giroux scream, she who used to give me *croquignoles* years ago, when I was a boy, and I go to the rescue. I save the life of Jean Baptiste because of a *croquignole*. Also, it is a pity to let a strong man be choked in that black smoke, without a struggle, without a chance. I prefer to see him die fighting, so I pull him out of the fire that I may prolong the game. You understand, my gentle aunt, the ways of the tiger, which are those of his first cousin, the domestic cat?"

"Yes, I understand perfectly. The same family—a difference in size, that is all. We will play with him for a while, and then we will make an end. But first, my nephew, we have our little plan."

"Damn your little plan, you she-devil! We will speak of it to-morrow. Good-night, my blessed aunt. Pleasant dreams."

CHAPTER XVIII

MICHEL

In St. Placide, as elsewhere, the habitants usually build their houses quite near to the main road, with a background of green fields, but scarcely a tree by the house to give shade in summer or to break the force of the wind in winter. It is an ancestral custom, perhaps, coming down from the time when there was danger from wild beasts, Indians and forest fires; or it may be that the good habitants do not value trees because they find them superfluous. City people love to surround their homes with lawns and trees, a sort of make-believe country, but in the true country they are in the way, occupying space that could be used for other purposes, and giving shade injurious to potatoes, turnips, onions, cabbages, and all the other useful products of the vegetable garden. In the mountain valleys, above all, good land is scarce, and it is wasteful to give it over to the growing of trees, which do well enough in the hills above and the swamps below. For firewood, trees are necessary, but for shade, what need? The warm, sunny days are all too few, in any case. As for beauty, what could be finer than a broad expanse of cultivated fields, sunny open spaces of green and yellow, with the dark forest all about, a lovely picture in a handsome frame?

Michel Gamache was no cultivator, and his thoughts

of trees were not those of a grower of cabbages. To him the forest was a place of refuge, and every tree a sentinel on guard. How faithful they were, those tall sentinels, always standing in their places, always interposing their bodies as a shield, always spreading their branches as a covering? He loved them, every one, the maples, the poplars, the birches; but most of all the pines, the spruces, the balsams, and all the tribe of evergreens, that protected him against the summer's heat and the winter's cold and were a barrier between him and the outer world. They were good companions, too, for they talked with him in a language that he well understood, music that caused his heart-strings to vibrate, and awoke responsive echoes in his soul. In all the changing seasons, when the wind blew and when the air was still, in sunshine and rain, by night and by day, he loved to be in the forest, to see the varied forms, colours, and movements of the trees, to hear their voices, to converse with them without reserve, to be silent and to know that they were his friends. Yet he was no misanthrope, this strange man, but a lonely spirit whom the neighbours could not understand, and who felt most at home in the company of trees.

The neighbours seldom visited Michel Gamache, for they feared him, and it was a long and lonely path that led to his log castle in the forest. He was known as a wise man, one who had insight into the ways of the world and the hearts of men; could predict the weather and read the signs of the times; understood the medicinal virtues of all plants; was on friendly terms with all beasts, birds, and fishes; had sources of information unknown to the generality of men; could give advice that would heal the sick, discover lost property, unite estranged friends, and lead the distressed and perplexed into the way of prosperity and peace.

He was a sorcerer, who had sold his soul to Satan for a great treasure of gold; who never went to Mass nor confessed to the priest; who was often changed into a *loup garou;* who could cause cows to drop their calves, to withhold their milk, to become frantic and run away into the forest. He had the fatal gift of the evil eye; could bring the itch, the measles, the small-pox, and disease of every other kind; in short, he could command all the powers of darkness to torment and destroy his enemies, if only he wished to do so. Fortunately he had seldom, if ever, used this malignant power; and could usually be propitiated by a small offering, which, strange to say, he always refused. It was part of his contract with Satan, it would seem, that he should give his most valuable advice for nothing; though why the evil one should have made a stipulation so favourable to the neighbours it was hard to understand. Possibly Michel thought to save himself some of the pains of Purgatory by works of charity; but he should know that it was not a question of Purgatory any more when one had sold oneself to Satan, who would come some time, unexpected and unwelcome, and drag the lost soul down to the bottomless pit, where works of charity were of no avail and indulgence was unknown.

It was terrible, no doubt, the fate of a sorcerer, and dangerous to have communications with him; but what was one to do when in great trouble and all other means had failed, when the priest could not help and the saints gave no heed? Surely the good God would forgive poor people who, in their extremity, sought aid from such a source. Besides, some said that

Michel was no sorcerer at all, but a practiser of white magic, a familiar of good spirits, and that they who consulted him were in no sense tainted with the sin of witchcraft. Surely it was right to give the old man the benefit of the doubt. Anyway, one could confess and receive absolution, for Father Paradis had never accused Michel of witchcraft, but only of neglecting his religious duties; and had always let the penitents off with reproof and warning and a penance not too severe.

Jean Baptiste laughed at all this idle talk; yet in the hour of loss and disappointment he turned, not to the priest, the professional confessor, but to his friend and his father's friend, the old man who had known defeat and humiliation, but had gained wisdom and strength, a true appreciation of the values of life, a high courage in danger, and a joyful hope toward the future that rested in the good will of God. If any man could give advice at such a time it was Michel Gamache; but in any case he would understand, and it would be a great relief and satisfaction to tell him everything, to show him the destruction and ruin that had come, to consider what material should be cast away, and what could be used again in making a new building out of the wreckage of the past.

So Jean Baptiste, on the evening after the great fire, when the benumbing effect of the calamity was over and he had come to realize the full magnitude of the disaster, betook himself to the forest retreat of Michel Gamache.

Michel, who was sitting on the doorstep, heard Jean coming along the winding path, and rose to meet him as he came out into the open.

"Good evening, Jean," he said, "I was expecting you."

"Yes," said Jean, "I would come to you, of course."

"Of course," said Michel, nodding his head. "You are in trouble."

"Do you not know, Monsieur Gamache, that my house is gone, burned to the ground? You have been away, then."

"Yes, I have been away for some time, at Lac Desir, up there. I was arranging my camp for the winter. There will be good trapping this season, better than ever. Oh, the prospects are good, excellent. Come with me, Jean; we shall both become quite rich. A single skin of the silver fox, as you know, may be worth a thousand dollars, or more. There will be caribou without limit, and moose; not to mention hares and grouse, so that we shall not lack for food. With a few bags of flour and some sides of bacon we shall live like lords, better than the guests of the Hotel St. Louis, I assure you. And oh, the freedom, the glory of that life, far from the world, near to Nature and to God! It would be a good place for you, Jean, for a time—a retreat, you know. At times people need that, my son, for the soul's rest. But your house is gone, you say? Well, that was to be expected."

"Expected?"

"Assuredly, my son. Did I not warn you? No! Well, it could not have been prevented. Pamphile Lareau is here, is he not?"

"Pamphile? Do you know, Monsieur Gamache, that he saved my life at the risk of his own?"

"Yes, I know. Which proves, does it not, that he started the fire?"

"Started the fire? Impossible! It was the lightning."

"You think so, Jean, but you are mistaken. Listen. Last evening at midnight I was at my cabin at Lac Desir, thirty miles away, sitting on a log near the door and looking out on the lake—a mirror in which all the stars were reflected. Not a cloud was in the sky. Suddenly there was a flash, as of lightning, and there, in the middle of the lake, stood La Folie; and on the top of the roof lay Jean Baptiste Giroux, yourself, pale as one who is dead. Then the brightness was gone, but still the shadow of the house was on the lake, and would not go away. After a time a light appeared in the window, then a burst of flame; and I saw the people running out of the door, climbing from the windows, the neighbours arriving, with much excitement and confusion and wild gesticulation. But still the body of Jean Baptiste, your body, lay upon the roof, until Pamphile arrived and you were saved. Yes, I saw it all, as in the depths of a crystal. Did I see Pamphile kindle the fire? No, for it was quite dark, you know; but that he did it I have no doubt. It was not the lightning; therefore it was Pamphile. So I knew that you would need me, and I came. Thirty miles through the forest would be a good walk even for a young fellow like you, would it not?"

"Indeed it would, Monsieur Gamache, and I thank you for coming. It does me good to talk with you. Already I begin to take courage, to make new plans, to see light ahead. But as to Pamphile, surely you are mistaken. At great risk he led me down from the burning roof. It was the act of a hero, and I have a mind to forgive him for everything—for burning the house, even, if he really did it."

"Forgive him if you like, Jean, but watch him all the

same. Yes, it will be worth while to watch Pamphile and that witch, Mère Tabeau. They have other plans, without doubt. The fire was only a beginning. Pamphile would kill you, Jean, if he could."

"This is interesting, Monsieur Gamache. You make me forget, almost, the loss of my house, and my other troubles."

"Other troubles, Jean? What are they, my son? But I know without asking, and I tell you that there is no cause for trouble. She loves you."

"No, Monsieur Gamache. On the contrary, she has gone to the convent; for she does not love me, nor anything in the kingdom of earth. It is the heavenly kingdom that she desires, and the good God whom she loves."

"Do not believe it, Jean," said the old man, with an inscrutable smile. "It is you only that she loves; and if she thinks of the religious life it is because of love —and pride. But love is stronger than pride. To what convent, Jean?"

"The Ursulines, Monsieur Gamache."

"The Ursulines. Well, that is not so bad. Teaching sisters. That is not to throw away one's life altogether. They are good ladies, those sisters of Ste. Ursule. She will be happy there, after a time, after she has forgotten. But to forget—there is the difficulty. Has Mother Sainte Anne forgotten, I wonder?"

"Mother Sainte Anne?"

"Only an acquaintance of former days, Jean, a friend of forty years ago. But have courage, my son. Gabrielle has not yet taken the veil, has not even begun the novitiate. The bride of Heaven? No, no! For a young girl of such accomplishments, of a beauty so rare, of an affection so tender, it was a sad mistake. How I would have cherished her! How she would have adorned the home, brightened the fireside! And the children that might have played about, sat upon one's knee, thrown their arms about one's neck! *Mon Dieu! Mon Dieu!* What a mistake!"

"Monsieur!"

"Jean!"

"You are not speaking of Gabrielle."

"Of Gabrielle? No. Yes. She will be all this to you, and more. Have courage, my friend."

"Monsieur Gamache, you are a true friend, one who stands by in the hour of need. Those dark clouds are passing away now, and the sky is clearing, with the promise of a fine day to-morrow. Good night, Monsieur, and thank you a thousand times."

"Wait, Jean. You have not spoken of the house."

"The house? Oh, I had forgotten that. It is not of much consequence, by comparison. Indeed, I am almost glad that it is gone. Yet it is a great loss, a calamity."

"And the debt, Jean?"

"The debt. Yes, that is still worse. Bonhomme Laroche will try to take the farm, I fear—the old place where we have lived for so many years. For myself I should not care, but for the good mother it would be terrible."

"You are right, Jean. To the young such a calamity is nothing. They have good health, the strong arm, the cheerful spirit, the high courage, the undaunted will. Nothing can subdue them. They are downcast, for a time; but presently they rise again, stronger than ever, more eager for the struggle, the test of manhood. But with the old it is different. They have not the vigour, the joy of living any more; nor the elasticity of spirit that gives the rebound, the recovery. They fall, and remain on the ground; they are injured, and the wound does not heal; they are sick, and do not recover. No, Jean, the old are afflicted with an incurable disease. The joy of battle is not for them. For them sleep and rest—the sleep of death, the rest of the grave. Jean, the good mother must not leave the old home."

"No, Monsieur Gamache; it must not be. I will see to that."

"But how, Jean?"

"Oh, Monsieur, I will find a way, you may be sure. For one thing, Bonhomme the miser cannot claim his principal—that will not be due for two years. He can demand only the interest, a trifling sum, after all. Meanwhile the farm is there, and I shall have the mail contract and some tourists. In winter there will be lumbering or the trapping of which you speak. When I think of silver foxes at a thousand dollars apiece I see the debt vanish in a single season. Oh, we are not ready to die yet, by any means. A man of my size and strength can surely earn a living for the good mother and pay the debt off as well. Do not fear, Monsieur Gamache."

"I have no fear for you, Jean, no fear at all. But come with me—I have something to show you."

Michel led the way into the cabin, a habitation of a single long room, with a fireplace and the apparatus of a kitchen at one end, and the furniture of a bedroom at the other. It was the abode of a hunter and fisherman, yet everything was neat and proper as though cared for by the hand of a woman. On the walls were guns, fishing-rods, and snowshoes; the antlers of caribou, moose, and red deer; a snowy owl; a golden eagle; with various quaint decorations in shells and porcupine quills after the manner of the Montaignais Indians. On the floor were the tanned skins of bear, wolves, and lynxes; while over the fireplace, like the holy picture of a shrine, hung a water-colour by a famous artist—the portrait of a young and beautiful woman.

" There, Jean, my son, son of my old friend Toussaint Giroux, behold that picture! You have seen it before, but do you know who it is? No; but I will tell you. It is Mademoiselle Annette Duval, formerly of the parish of Chateau Richer, now Mother Sainte Anne of the Ursulines, the patron saint of this retreat, the holy angel who protects this place, who presides over this home. You have said that Mademoiselle Gabrielle is with her. Well, she is in good company, and will receive the best of advice. Have courage, my friend. Mother Sainte Anne is religious, without doubt, but something more than that. Beneath the robe of religion there beats still a woman's heart. I have not seen her in forty years, but I know that those eyes have the same gentle gaze, those lips the same lovely smile, and that day and night she prays for one whom once she loved."

Michel stood in silence for some moments as one who prayed, and then turned suddenly to Jean with a dramatic gesture and an air of cheerfulness, almost of gaiety.

" Well, Jean Baptiste, did I bring you here to worship at the shrine of a bygone generation? By no means. It was to solve the problem of your life, to untangle the complication of your affairs, to put you on the road to fortune, fame, and love. To that end I will reveal to you the secret which I have guarded for forty years. You look incredulous, my friend, but you shall see and believe. Remove that bearskin, if you please. Yes, the big one in the centre of the room. You see that trap-door with the iron ring? Take hold and lift. Heavy? Only a hundred pounds or so—a mere trifle for a man like you. Now let us descend. We will take one of the candles from the altar—no sacrilege in a cause like this. Come on, Jean. Now we can see better, as our eyes become accustomed to the gloom. Do you see the old iron box in the corner over there—there where it has rested so many years? It is ten years since I examined it, but there is no reason to think that it has been disturbed in all that time. *Dieu*, if it has been touched! But no, it is covered with the dust of many years. Lift the lid. You cannot? No, for it is locked. Do not be impatient—it was only a little joke of mine. Here is the key. Turn it once—twice. There, you have it. Open now, and look—look!"

"*Mon Dieu!*" said Jean, as he knelt by the box, and eagerly scanned the contents. "What a quantity of gold! Napoleons, sovereigns, and some Spanish coins of fifty years ago. A treasure, a great treasure! The box is not large, but heavy. Let us try. *Sapré*, but it weighs four or five hundred pounds, at the very least. It would take a strong man to carry it away, but a burglar might pick the lock. Lucky that there are no such people in St. Placide. Still, Monsieur Gamache, I recommend that you place this money in the bank at Quebec. It has been safe for forty years, but I should fear to leave it here for a single night. But what a treasure! I begin to believe that you are a sorcerer after all, and that these piles of yellow coin are devil's gold."

" Nothing of the sort!" exclaimed the old man, in high glee. " It is all good money of the mints of France and England, good yellow gold, receivable anywhere in the world. And what is more, Jean, my son, it belongs to you."

" To me, Monsieur Gamache? Impossible! Certainly not!"

" But yes, Jean, it was your father's, and now it is yours."

" My father's? How can that be? He was always a poor man."

" His own fault, Jean, when he had a treasure like this. You, I hope, will not be so foolish. It is yours, as I have said. Be so good as to take it away."

" But why did not my father take it?"

" Why? Why? How do I know? Because, because your father was the biggest damn fool that I have ever known. He was a fool, I say, and I was another. We were two fools, two drivelling idiots. Be wise, Jean, and ask no more questions. It is good gold, yellow gold, coin of the realm, receivable for all debts, bankable anywhere in the world, of unquestioned value. What more do you want?"

" Only one question, Monsieur Gamache. Why then did my father refuse to take it?"

" *Peste!*" exclaimed Michel, stamping his foot. " This is the old man again, a chip from the old block; yes, the old blockhead himself. Well, if you will have it, I will tell you. It was a treasure that we found in the hulk of a ship half-buried in the sands of Anticosti. There were no names, no papers, only the bones of some men along the shore with some fragments of clothing—that was all. The wreck we burned; the bones we buried in the sand; and the gold we took to Ste. Famille on the Isle of Orleans—that is to say, it was I who took it?"

"And my father?"

"Refused to take it—would not touch a single piece."

"No?"

"No! Because, as he said, they were smugglers or pirates, those men who had been cast away; and the gold was the reward of robbery, or the price of blood. Yes, he said, in the very words that you have used, that it was devil's gold. He would have given it to the Church, that the altar might sanctify the gift, as he said; but I would not. No, and I left it buried for forty years. Devil's gold? What folly! Yes, he was a valiant man, that Toussaint Giroux, a valiant man and a trusty friend; but obstinate as a mule."

"Devil's gold!" repeated Jean, slowly. "The reward of robbery. The price of blood. Yes, that was it, a treasure acquired by fraud or force, jetsam that one may not own, but may dedicate to a holy purpose. He was a valiant man, that good father, as you have said. He would not touch the treasure, and I, his son, will not touch it either."

Michel held up the candle and passed it slowly before the face of Jean Baptiste, but could find in the firm mouth and steady eye no sign of relenting. Then, with a shrug of the shoulders, he said, as though reciting an oft-repeated formula:

"It would be useless, no doubt, to remind you that you are throwing away a fortune, that you are allowing a mass of wealth to lie idle that might start a great enterprise and give work to a thousand men. It would be in vain to tell you that you are giving up all your plans for the improvement of the parish; that you are sacrificing your mother and the girl you love; that you are blighting your life, blasting your prospects, and shutting the door of opportunity in your face. That is, in substance, what I said to Toussaint Giroux; that is what I say to Jean Baptiste, his youngest son— and with the same effect."

"The same," said Jean Baptiste.

"Then I have to tell you, Jean, that you are the same species of fool as your father. What a damn fool he was, that man! I rejoice to think of it. What courage! What determination! What resolve! A hero, a knight without fear and without reproach. Such a man was your father, Jean, my son. Never forget it! Jean Baptiste, son of Toussaint Giroux, I salute you!"

CHAPTER XIX

MOTHER SAINTE ANNE

IT was about four o'clock in the afternoon, and the shadows of the tall houses of the Rue des Jardins reached already the middle of the narrow street, as an old gentleman in the garb of half a century ago passed along the shady side and entered the open gate of the Ursuline Convent. He was a tall man, not handsome, but of an erect bearing and distinguished appearance; and the fashion of his frock coat of fine homespun, his beaver hat and black stock, together with his carefully trimmed grey hair and whiskers, proclaimed him a country dandy of a former generation, dressed for Church, or to pay a visit of importance to his lady love.

It was more than forty years since he had last paid such a visit, and the costume of that occasion had reposed in the bottom of an old cedar box during all those years. But now he wore it with pride and dignity; and carried his light malacca cane with something of the swagger of former days, when he had thought himself as good as any of the young bloods of Quebec, not excepting the army officers, who trusted overmuch in the grandeur of their red uniforms to win the ladies' hearts. Was he not a cadet of a good family; son of the seigneur of Ste. Famille on the Island; and had he not the right to hold up his head among the best? Indeed, whether he had the right or not, he was accustomed to do so by virtue of his consciousness of personal merit and his strong right hand. Evidently, the old gentleman had been a force to be reckoned with; and even now the memory of a bygone glory seemed to linger about him, commanding the respect and deference of all the passers-by.

Crossing the paved courtyard with an active stride remarkable in one of his years, he pulled the door-bell and waited until the portress came, a sister of mature age and sober mien.

"May I have the honour of an interview with the Reverend Mother Superior?"

The sister hesitated.

"It is somewhat unusual," she began, but immediately added: "I dare say that the Reverend Mother will see you. Will Monsieur be so kind as to give his name?"

The old gentleman presented a thin visiting-card, and was shown into the waiting-room with the intimation that the Reverend Mother would soon appear. The room was plainly furnished; with a carpet of dull colours, a few straight-backed chairs, and a plain walnut table on which were some religious books—the *Spiritual Exercises of Saint Ignace*, the *Imitation of Christ*, a Roman Breviary in four volumes, and a life of Angèle de Brescia. On the bare walls was a large crucifix, and a number of holy pictures representing the Lord Jesus, the Holy Mother, Sainte Ursule, and other saints and martyrs, both men and women; who for the love of God had forsaken parents and friends, abjured the world, crucified the flesh, and given themselves a living sacrifice unto God. It was an exhibition of piety such as might well make one regret the struggles and sins of the outer world, admire the sincerity and devotion of those who had chosen the way of the Cross, and rejoice in the thought that they were now singing the eternal song around the throne of God.

As the old man stood looking at the ascetic and courageous faces, the spirit of the place came stealing upon him; and he saw that there was a way of life in which the lonely, the loveless, the defeated and disappointed, as well as men and women of high ideals and lofty purposes, might find refuge, shelter, companionship, and peace, and have at the same time work to do that would give scope to all their powers and absorb all their thoughts. They would suffer, no doubt, but not more than others; while they would have great satisfaction in the success of their work and the triumph of their cause. It was a good life in itself for those who had the vocation; and as for the final reward there was a wonderful hope, a glorious chance, for which sane people might well throw down the vain baubles and frivolities of the world. Yes, the religious life was not to be despised. Only human love was lacking, but what was that? A passing fancy, the pastime of an hour.

"Monsieur Gamache."

The old gentleman turned from the holy pictures to find the Reverend Mother Superior standing before him, a little old lady clad in the garb of the Ursulines, with a rosary of plain jet beads about her neck, from which hung an ivory crucifix, yellow with age. Her sweet, wistful face was pale, but she smiled, and her eyes glistened as she held out her hand to the old friend.

He bent over the frail little hand and raised it to his lips in the old courtly way. As for words, he could find none.

"Be seated, Monsieur," said Mother Sainte Anne, taking up the thread of conversation dropped so many years ago. "It is a great pleasure to see you again, and all the more so because quite unexpected. 'Until to-morrow,' you said, as we parted that day. I remember it well. A good many to-morrows have come and gone since that time. Yet I should have known you anywhere. It is I who have changed the more."

"But no, Annette—pardon me, Reverend Mother—I do not find that you have changed in the least."

The Mother Superior smiled, and a faint blush appeared on her pale cheeks.

"In one respect you have not changed, Monsieur Gamache—you were always able to turn a compliment in a very pleasant way, though without much regard to fact, perhaps. It is sinful; yet one likes to hear those charming little untruths, which flatter but do not deceive. You shall confess to Father Félix, Monsieur, and he will give you a suitable penance."

"Confess, Reverend Mother? To what end? That is what I have not done in forty years. There, I am confessing now, and already I feel better. You have power to grant absolution, have you not?"

Mother Sainte Anne held up her hands in amazement and horror.

"Forty years! You have not confessed once in all that time, since, since—— *Bon Dieu*, what neglect! What a sin against the soul, against the spirit of God! If you had died thus, would any prayers, my prayers, or those of your guardian angel, even, have been able to deliver you? Oh, Monsieur Gamache, Michel, my old friend, delay no longer, not a single day. The grace of God is everlasting, inextinguishable. It still pursues you; and by my voice it once more asks you to confess, to demand forgiveness, to receive absolution."

The Reverend Mother was weeping, and Michel Gamache was not unmoved. Yet he could not at once rid himself of the cynicism of years, but allowed himself to doubt his best friend.

" Is it that you ask this as a personal request, Reverend Mother, or merely to save another soul from Hell?"

" Michel," said the old lady, in a low voice, " I have not seen you once since the day we parted, but during every day in all those years I have wished, yes, I have prayed that we might meet again in the eternal world."

" Why then, Annette, did you leave me at that time, without a word?"

" Michel," she replied, in a broken voice, " they told me that you had gone away in anger, and afterwards that you were dead. It was not for years, when it was too late, that I learned the truth."

" Annette," said the old man, " I was always sure that there was some mistake; and always have I thought of you with the same regard, a love that will last until the end of life, and afterwards, whether in Heaven or Hell, will remain the same."

" Michel, it is good to hear you talk like that, for now I know that we shall meet again in the homeland of the soul. You will go to Father Félix, will you not, this very day? You will find him in the Basilica an hour before sunset, in the little box to the right as you enter the main door. You will see him ? "

" At least I will visit Father Paradis at St. Placide immediately after my return."

" No, Michel, do not delay. You will find Father Félix to-day, will you not, for my sake ? "

" Yes, Annette, I will do it for your sake—and my own."

" Michel, you make me very happy," said Annette, in words that Michel had heard before, in the old days. " I have transgressed, I fear, the rules of the convent, and I also shall have confessions to make. But I am glad that you have come, and Father Félix will understand."

" Yes, he will understand, no doubt, if he is still a man. The priests, fortunately, are human beings like ourselves; and have the same temptations, the same sufferings. Who could confess to an angel who has never passed through the human life ? But the priests, the saints, the Holy Mother, the Lord Jesus—they know, they understand. And you, Reverend Mother, will understand when I present a petition in favour of my friend, my son, I may say—Jean Baptiste Giroux, of our parish."

" Jean Baptiste Giroux ? I do not know of him. He is a son, perhaps, of your ancient friend Toussaint Giroux, of Chateau Richer, whom I have seen in former times. He was a noble young man, I have heard."

" Yes, Reverend Mother, and the son is like his father, tall, strong, courageous, with all the virtues, all the abilities. But for all that, one whom he loves has left him, and will give herself to the religious life."

" And why not, Monsieur Gamache ? "

" Why not, you say ? How can you say that,

Annette ? Will it not be a mistake, a sad mistake, as in our case ?"

"Oh!" exclaimed Mother Sainte Anne, with a catch in her voice. "Was it for this you came ? Well, it will be useless, I fear. Mademoiselle Taché will take the first vows very soon, and after that it is not likely that she will change her mind. She will be a notable addition to our Congregation—a young lady of good family, beautiful, accomplished, vivacious, of a charming disposition, of a most ardent devotion, and with a considerable dowry. Yes, that is not to be despised, the dowry which the bride of Heaven brings to her Lord and Master, a gift to lay at His feet, a contribution to the great work of the Church through the humble sisters of Sainte Ursule. Yes, Monsieur, Mademoiselle Taché will be happy and useful with us. She is in every way fitted for the religious vocation, and as a teaching sister will be one of the best. Many heretics are won to the true fold through teachers such as she. Yes, I foretell great things for her. A true vocation."

"A vocation ? Reverend Mother, can you believe it ?"

"But certainly. Who could doubt it ? She has all the qualities, all the marks, and she wishes it sincerely."

"Are you certain, quite certain ?"

"Of course," replied the old lady, with some asperity. "Has she not said so ?"

"But, Reverend Mother, permit a single question. Does she know that Jean Baptiste loves her, with his whole heart, without reserve ? Does she know this, or does she think that he has forsaken her, that he despises her, that he is in love with another ?"

"How should I know, Monsieur? Mademoiselle Taché has been very reserved on this point. There has been some affair of the heart—that is all that I know."

"Reverend Mother," said the old man, rising. "Grant me but one favour for the sake of old times. Be so kind as to tell Mademoiselle Gabrielle what I have said."

"I will tell her, of course, but it will make no difference. Those who are called to the religious life are inspired by a love that is higher than any mere human emotion. It is a live coal from the altar of God, a spark of that love which brought the divine Saviour to earth to live and die for a lost world. And when one thus gives oneself in the spirit of true devotion, one finds a peace and rest which the world cannot give, and bliss ineffable on the bosom of the divine Redeemer. In our love for Him and for His cause all human loves are embraced and glorified—we give them up that we may receive them again, purified and transfigured, in the beauty of holiness. Ah, Monsieur, the religious life is a good life ; and afterwards, in the eternal world, the faithful will live with God unto the ages of the ages. Amen !"

"Amen !" said the old man, solemnly. "Give unto them eternal rest, O God ; and may perpetual light illumine them !"

"Adieu, Annette," said Michel, a moment later. "It has been good to see you again."

"Yes, and for me also," said Mother Sainte Anne. "But tell me, Michel. Did you come for the sake of your young friend only, or for Gabrielle?"

"No, Annette. It was for your sake most of all. I

have been on the point of coming for many years, and the other motive was the occasion, the pretext, merely."

Mother Sainte Anne's face lighted up with a radiant smile ; and through a mist of tears Michel Gamache saw again the youth and loveliness of former years, and was satisfied.

CHAPTER XX

THE ROBBERY

"THERE, my nephew," said Mère Tabeau, as the two emerged from the forest surrounding the log castle of Michel Gamache. "Behold the den of the beast. He has gone away for a day or two, permitting us to make a little exploration. Very considerate of him, was it not ?"

"But there is nobody here—no dog, even."

"No, my good nephew, not even a dog. It is a sorcerer, the inhabitant of this place, a species of wolf, you know; and wolves have no love for dogs. There are no domestic animals of any kind; and no wild beasts either, except the sorcerer himself and some of his cousins, who come from the forest now and then."

"Wolves ?" exclaimed Pamphile.

"Even so," she sneered. "But do not fear, my brave nephew; they spend the day in the recesses of the forest, and do not come out until the evening twilight. Fear nothing."

"Bah!" said Pamphile. "I have no fear of people, nor dogs, nor even wolves. If they were here there would be something to kill. No, my aunt, it is not wolves that I fear, but this damned silence. There is not the call of a bird, the chatter of a squirrel, nor the chirp of an insect. Even the leaves of the trees are still. It is a silence that one can hear. It is as though it were a place of the dead. My aunt, it would be better, I think, to go away."

The old crone laughed in scorn, a shrill, cackling laugh that woke the echoes of the forest.

"There!" she said. "You hear something, do you not? Bah! You surprise me, Monsieur the bravo of Nevada. One who carries a pistol, one who has fought with savages, cowboys, cattle-thieves, gamblers, one who has saved his enemy from a burning house— to be afraid of a silence, and in broad daylight! It is to laugh. Ha! Ha! Ho! Ho! Well, let us go away. Let us leave the treasure, and the old miser will give it to Jean Baptiste. *Hein?* You don't like that?"

"*Sacré!*" said Pamphile. "He shall not have it, that proud one, that peasant with the swagger of a grand seigneur, that bishop that was to be. He despises me, does he? He strikes me with a whip, like a dog. Sacred pig's head! I will see him crawl in the dust, and then I will crush him with my foot. Obtain the treasure, he? Come on, my aunt; let us storm the castle. Shall we break down the door or cut out a window? The door is on the latch, you say—not barred? *Mon Dieu!* Is it possible? A treasure in such a place, and no bolt, no bar, no guard? My aunt, it is a trap. You shall press the latch; you shall open the door; and then you shall receive a charge of buckshot in the body. No, the game is not worth the candle."

"Coward!" snarled the old hag. "Good-for-nothing! Call yourself a man! Get out of my way, you chicken-liver, you who have not the spirit of a mouse! There! I open the door; I enter the den; the beast is not there; there is no gun, no trap, no weapon of any kind but what you see on the walls, in full view. Now you can arm yourself to the teeth, if you like; but there is no need. Oh yes, I have been here before, to make a reconnaissance, so to speak; and I would have taken the treasure myself, but that it is too heavy. You will have trouble to lift it, my nephew. But you are strong, Pamphile, as strong as Jean Baptiste himself, if you would believe it. You could kill him— you. I say it, I, your mother."

"What? What are you saying, my aunt?"

"No aunt at all, Pamphile—your mother, sure enough, your dear mother. Kiss me, my son."

"Wait, my aunt; this is too sudden. My mother? Is it possible? A most affectionate mother, I must say—a species of ostrich, or alligator. Well, since you say it, you who should know, I must believe, I suppose; but I confess that I am not so very proud of the relationship. And my father, what of him? Perhaps you can reveal this also, since you are telling things."

"Well, that is not so easy to determine; but there is reason to think that it is Monsieur the lord of this castle, the owner of the treasure that we are to take."

"Michel Gamache?"

"No other."

"Then, my aunt, my mother, if you will, the treasure is ours, in a sense."

"That is what I have been trying to say."

"Well, my sainted parent; let us take what is ours before the old man returns. He is a miser, as is well known; an unnatural father, as you have intimated; a rascal in any case. That he is a sorcerer I no longer believe, for the species of sorcery which he practises is no mystery to me. I have used it, many a time, back there in Nevada. No, my dear parents, let us not fool one another any more, for we are all sorcerers together. Dog does not eat dog, as you know. Curious, that fear that I had a moment since. It is all gone now; driven away by the power of reason and a revelation concerning family ties. Come, my lovely mother; let us find the treasure and take it away without delay."

"Pamphile, you are a strange mixture of philosopher and fool, coward and hero; but that is what one should expect from the events connected with your birth. Some time I will tell you the story, but now we have other fish to fry. Kick away those skins. There is the trap-door. Lift it. Let us descend. A candle? I have it. Follow me. Now we are in the cave, and over there in the corner we should find the box. There it is. *Dieu merci!* You can lift it, of course. Take it up, now, and carry it out. I will help you, if necessary. I am not very strong, but for a treasure like this I could put forth some effort yet. Think of it, Pamphile, the pleasure of counting all that gold, of feeling the weight of every piece, of seeing the glimmer of it by the light of a candle. I, too, must have a cave, a dark cave with no windows; and every night I will descend to look, and feel and count. It will cost something for candles, but one cannot have pleasure without expense. As for you, Pamphile, you will want to spend your share, to gamble it away; and soon you will have nothing, nothing. What a pity! Better leave it all with me."

"When you are tired of talking, my dear mother, will you be so good as to give me the key?"

"The key? I have no key. That is what I have not been able to find. But you can carry the box, I know."

"There is no need for that, my precious mother. If

I had a piece of strong wire. Ah, here it is in my pocket. A happy accident, is it not? How useful pockets are! Possibly we might find some other useful articles there, if the lock should prove refractory—a stick of dynamite, for example. It is an interesting trade, the locksmith's, one of the accomplishments that I have learned in the course of my wanderings. But this is not a difficult combination. There goes one bolt; and there goes the other. Now the hasp is loose, and the lid is ready to open. If there is to be an explosion it will come at this stage. My cherished parent, you shall have the pleasure of opening the treasure chest, since you have desired it for so many years. The old can be spared, you know, but the future of the world is with the young."

"Bah!" said the old woman. "You make a great fuss about nothing, my brave son; you with the long legs, the broad shoulders, the fierce look, the big words. Bah! You are a poor excuse for a man. I will lift the lid, of course, and you shall see what we have come to find. There! Look now! Look! Oh, *Mon Dieu! Mon Dieu!* What is this? *Sacré diable! Mille cochons! Sacré! Sacré! Cru-ru-ru-ru-de Dieu!*"

"What is the matter?" cried Pamphile. "What the deuce is here? No gold, eh? I thought as much. Stones from the river? Yes, better than I expected. Oh, be still, you old fool. Stop your yelling. Who is making a fuss now, I should like to know? Be still, I say!"

"Oh, Pamphile! Oh! Oh! You do not know, you cannot imagine the disappointment, the sorrow, after all these years, to see all my hopes, all my plans, come to an end like this. No treasure, no revenge!

Ah, the miserable one, to rob a poor woman, a poor old woman who had but one hope, one ambition, one thing to make life worth while! Now all is gone. No money, no revenge! Nothing, nothing! *Sacré! Sacré!* Pamphile, I am finished. Let us go, my nephew."

"Nephew?" said Pamphile, as they slowly mounted the steps to the floor above. "I was your son a moment since, although I did not believe it for a moment."

"It was a lie, Pamphile. You are my nephew, truly, the son of my sister Cécile. She was a fool, Cécile, and I could not abide her. Oh, we were two doves—Cécile and Celestine—two angels with downy wings. Your father? He also was a fool. What he could see in Cécile I could not guess. They went away without my blessing, you may be sure, and soon after he got himself drowned in the Gatineau. Oh, they were married with all regularity in the church, by a priest—Father Gibaut of Chateau Richer. No, you are no son of Michel Gamache, that traitor, that thief! Ah, if I had him here I would stab him to the heart, that he might be damned for ever, body and soul. I would go to Hell myself, to see him burn. A thousand devils take him, stick him on forks, tear his eyes out, his tongue, his liver, roast him in the fire! Ha, you damned one, squirm, wriggle, writhe in the fire that never shall be quenched—for ever, for ever, unto the ages of the ages! Ah, that is revenge, revenge at last—sweet, sweet!"

Mère Tabeau was raving; and when she saw the picture of Annette Duval, serene and calm like a holy saint above an altar, she tore it from its place; spat upon it; stamped upon it; and then raged about the room like a wild beast, tearing and breaking, scratching and biting and foaming at the mouth; until at last she fell unconscious to the floor, and Pamphile carried her home.

Toward evening Mère Tabeau recovered consciousness, and asked for the priest, knowing that she had but a little while to live. Father Paradis came in haste, carrying the *Bon Dieu;* while Pamphile, who drove, kept ringing the warning bell; whereat all who heard fell on their knees to pray for the departing soul. The priest remained with the dying woman for a long time, hearing her last confession, administering the holy wafer, anointing with the holy oil, and offering prayers of intercession until the last breath was expired, the heart had ceased to beat, and the soul had passed away from the mortal body.

When Father Paradis came from the chamber of death there was upon his face an expression of ineffable peace, as of one in communion with the eternal world; and his eyes had the far-away look of one who gazes upon things unseen. Even Pamphile felt a sense of awe and mystery, and for some time drove on in silence. Then, unable to contain himself any longer, he broke out suddenly:

" She was a bad woman, Monsieur le curé."

" What ? What is that you say, Pamphile ? "

" She was a wicked old woman, and is now in Hell, no doubt."

" Ah, Pamphile, how do I know ? I am not her judge. She is in the hands of God."

" Yes, Monsieur le curé, but if there is a mortal sin which she has not committed I do not know what it is.

I understand that any one of these is enough to damn the soul. Is it not so?"

"Yes, Pamphile, if unforgiven. But who shall limit the mercy of God? Even Judas, if he had repented, might have been forgiven. This poor old woman, who has sinned and suffered, comes, like Magdalen, to the feet of Jesus; in repentance and with tears, confesses her sins and receives absolution. The thief on the cross——"

"Oh yes, I know," said Pamphile, "but is it possible to cheat God like that? The old reprobate lives in sin to the very last; and then, to crown all, performs an act of sublime hypocrisy, cheating herself, the priest, and Almighty God. If she had died in the fit—what then?"

"God was merciful to her, Pamphile. He knew the circumstances of her life, her parentage, associations, temptations. He knows all, comprehends all, and is able to forgive when we could not. God is our creator, my son; do not forget that; and is disposed to overlook the sins of His creatures, poor insects that we are. We do not cheat Him, no, but He makes allowance."

"Well, that is a comfortable faith, Monsieur le curé. I hope that the good God will make allowance for me too, for the little sins of the past, and for some that I intend to commit before I die."

"Pamphile!" said the priest, in horror. "That is little short of blasphemy; and approaches the sin against the Holy Spirit, for which there is no forgiveness, neither in this world nor in the world to come. No, my son, one must have the good intention, else one cannot receive the grace of forgiveness, because the heart is closed. Pamphile, my son, repent of the sins of the past; cast away the bad intention for the future; and open your heart to the grace of God. Now, my son, without delay."

"Ah, Monsieur, I wish to do so. Indeed, I have already commenced by giving up a little scheme of mine, the St. Ange Gold Mining Company, Limited, to which so many of our good friends have subscribed. But I will not take their money, for they need it more than I."

"God will reward you, Pamphile."

"I hope so, Monsieur Paradis."

"And if you have any other bad intention, Pamphile, cast it from you and you will have peace in your soul."

"I will, Monsieur, I will; but first I must settle a little score with one of the good neighbours."

"Forgive him, my son, as you hope to be forgiven."

"Impossible, Monsieur le curé. I will settle the score; and afterwards I will come and tell you, for I have long desired to turn over a new leaf. I might have been a good man, Monsieur; but I was turned in the wrong direction. You shall turn me the other way, Monsieur le curé."

"Now, Pamphile."

"To-morrow, Monsieur le curé."

"There may be no to-morrow, Pamphile."

"Well, Monsieur Paradis, I will take the risk of that. I was always a gambler. One more chance; one more throw! Fortune, life, eternity I will risk once more; and after that we shall see. *Au revoir*, Monsieur le curé. Will you not say a little prayer for my intention?"

"Assuredly Pamphile, but I implore——"

"*Au revoir*, Monsieur. Until to-morrow or the day after."

CHAPTER XXI

LOVE AND WAR

IT was early morning; and Jean Baptiste, before beginning the day's work, was walking slowly along the path where he had met Gabrielle and Pamphile, thinking of the beauty and joy that he had lost, and trying to reconstruct the pattern of his life out of the broken fragments that were left. His conversation with Michel Gamache had given him renewed hope and courage; but now that his friend and confessor was away, his thoughts went back to the day of calamity, and his feet turned to the path of disappointment and vain regret.

It was a lovely path; winding along through the woods in a little glen where the ground was all covered with ferns, the rocks with moss, and the trees with lichen; while a clear stream descended in a series of cascades, filling the air with the sound of falling water—a mournful accompaniment to the sad thoughts of Jean Baptiste. Had Gabrielle been there the music of the stream would have been gay as the morning song of love; but now it was like a dirge; and the lonely glen was as the valley of the shadow of death.

Few flowers were there: some white orchids; the green, rank arum with its bitter root; and the pale, dejected Indian pipe, the corpse-plant, smoked in ghostly pow-wows by Indians long since dead. In the spring the baneberry had been in flower; but now only the blood-red berries were left; and where the trillium had bloomed were only withered leaves, and a poisonous, purple fruit. The springtime of love was gone; and the fruition of summer brought nothing but disappointment and despair.

And yet, on the very spot where Jean had met and lost Gabrielle, he found a little plant with shining leaves, a delicate white flower, and long roots of golden thread running through the cool, black mould. The roots were bitter to the taste, but of a healing virtue, purifying to the blood; the trefoil was a holy sign, potent to drive away evil spirits; and the white flower was a symbol of hope, a promise of life and love. As Jean knelt to gather the little plant, its several virtues seemed to enter his body and soul, and he arose revived, purified, and encouraged, once more believing in himself, Gabrielle, the world, and God. He had drunk a bitter cup to the dregs, it seemed, yet he felt greatly strengthened. Dark clouds of doubt had hung over his soul; but now they were passing away; the silver lining was showing; the blue was appearing; and soon the bright sun would be shining in a clear sky. He had felt himself alone, deserted by lover and friend; but now it seemed as though all were returning, and Gabrielle herself could not be far away. He had been beset by foes, not knowing how to escape; but now he felt the glow of returning strength, the joy of coming victory; and he had it in his heart to thank his enemies for having set themselves against him. So Jean strode up the path, out of the dark valley of humiliation, toward the lookout point on the hill, into the light and warmth of the rising sun; and as he went he sang in a deep, resonant voice a brave song of life and death and war:

> "Malbrough s'en va-t-en guerre,
> Mironton, mironton, mirontaine;
> Malbrough s'en va-t-en guerre
> Ne sait quand reviendra,
> Ne sait quand reviendra,
> Ne sait quand reviendra."

At the top of the hill Jean suddenly ceased to sing; and stood gazing in astonishment at the figure of a woman in a white dress, with a white sunbonnet on her head, standing by the fence and looking out over the valley as though expecting some one.

"Gabrielle!"

There was no reply, but the vision was still there.

"Gabrielle! Is it you, dear? Speak to me!"

"No, it is not your dear Gabrielle, and I am sorry," replied the apparition, turning. "But is it true that I resemble her? I should be much pleased to think so."

"No. Yes, Mademoiselle Laroche," stammered Jean. "All woman look alike more or less. There is a resemblance, certainly, and it was heightened by the sunlight. I was dazzled on coming out of the woods."

"Indeed!" said Blanchette, with a grim smile. "You are more truthful than complimentary, Monsieur Giroux. I know very well that I have not a pretty face. It was my figure, then, that reminded you of Mademoiselle Gabrielle?"

"Yes, Mademoiselle."

"Bah! Jean, why lie any more? You know very well that Mademoiselle Taché is tall and slender; while I, my friend, am short and plump, though not exactly stout, as yet. Confess, now, that it was a mere illusion created by the thought. That of which one is thinking all the time one sees everywhere. Good philosophy, is it not?"

"Mademoiselle Blanchette, you are always right. For penetration of thought there is none that can compare with you."

"Now, Jean, that is better. There you strike a true note which finds response in my intellect, if not in my heart. Yes, in my heart as well, for I am conscious of a certain superiority there also. As for mere beauty, that will disappear with time; but truth and love, the virtues of the intellect and of the heart, will endure for ever. Yes, for ever, Monsieur Jean."

"I know it, Mademoiselle."

"And those who have the least beauty, they often can love the most."

"Yes, Mademoiselle."

"Yes, you say 'yes, yes' like a parrot. Why do you not utter your own thoughts? Why do you not say that you have no wish to be loved; that you desire only to love; to find some object, some perfection of beauty that absorbs you wholly, in the contemplation of which you are lost, so that you forget all else; are blind, deaf, dumb, even, in the presence of all others. Can you deny it, Monsieur Giroux?"

"No, Mademoiselle."

"And if that object were taken away, to Heaven, perhaps, or to a nunnery, which is the same thing, it would be for ever enshrined in your heart, and you would worship it until the end of life."

"Yes, Blanchette."

"And no second object could ever take the place of the first. There could be no second, Jean Baptiste."

"Blanchette, all that you have said is true. I will not deny it."

"It would be useless, Jean. You do not lie with any conviction, my friend. You are a man of sincerity and truth, such as the good God seldom finds in man, and in woman, never. What constancy! Listen. I will tell you a secret. No woman is worth it. We are not like that, we others. We have our preferences, of course, but when it comes to choosing, the case is otherwise. To prefer is one thing; to choose is altogether different. Do you grasp the distinction, Monsieur the scholar? For example, if we cannot have our first preference we take the second, or the third; and as to the religious life, that is fourth or fifth, possibly, according to circumstances. To be the bride of Heaven, Monsieur, is highly desirable for the salvation of the soul, if one cannot be the bride of some good, brave, strong man. For me, I also will be the bride of Heaven, if I must."

"Blanchette, my friend, my sister, tell me—do you think that she will return?"

Blanchette did not speak, but nodded her head emphatically.

"Why do you think so, Blanchette?"

"What a question!" exclaimed Blanchette, with indignation. "The young Apollo wishes an enumeration of his virtues, evidently. Well, he shall not have it from me. I have given you my opinion, have I not? As for reasons, I will merely say, as other women do: because. Is that sufficient?"

"It must be, since you say so; and I thank you more than I can tell. And now I must leave you, I fear. There is work to do at the place—especially since the fire. We are making a new start, you know. Good-bye, Blanchette, I am glad that you were here."

"Must you go, Jean?"

"Yes. The sun is rising high, as you see. *Au revoir*, Blanchette."

"Wait a moment, Jean. Do not return by the path. Take the road, rather."

"Why then? It is much shorter by the path, and I must hasten. Good-bye again."

"Jean!"

"What is it, Blanchette?"

"Do not go that way."

"But why not?"

"Because."

"Because? You are laughing at me."

"No laughing matter, Jean. Do not go, I say."

"Blanchette, this is too foolish. I will go, of course."

"There may be danger."

"Danger?"

"Yes. Now I have said it. There is danger, Jean."

"That is interesting. Now I shall certainly go. I should like very much to find a little danger, to begin the day. Life was becoming too monotonous, altogether. Where is the danger, Blanchette?"

"In the glen, Jean, where the path crosses the little stream. Ah, now I have told you, and you will go. I do not wish you to be killed, Jean."

"Killed? Who would kill me, and why?"

"They do not wish to kill you, but merely to punish you."

"Punish me? That is good. But who, then?"

"Tom Sullivan and Paddy Brady."

"Ha! Ha! They have tried it before."

"And Pamphile."

"*Hein?* Three of them? Well, we must see about that. *Au revoir*, Blanchette. I shall be all right."

"Jean!"

"What then?"

"Do not kill him."

"Certainly not. Reassure yourself, Blanchette. Nobody will be killed."

"Jean! Jean!" called Blanchette, in distress; but he was already out of sight, hastening with eager steps toward the place of danger.

At the stream he stopped and looked about in all directions, but could see no one; and was passing along, disappointed but watchful, on the other side, where the path skirted a great rock, when two men stepped out and stood facing him in the middle of the way. They were Tom Sullivan and Pamphile Lareau.

"Good morning, gentlemen," said Jean, without slackening his pace, but turning aside to give them the path.

"Not so fast," said Pamphile, placing himself directly in front of Jean. "Stop a moment, if you please. We wish to talk to you."

"Certainly," replied Jean, stopping within arm's length of the two men, and measuring them with his eye. "But you will first throw away that pistol, my friend. You will not need it, I assure you."

"No, we shall not need it," said Pamphile, with a harsh laugh, throwing the weapon aside. "Two to one are odds enough, Jean Baptiste."

"Three to one would be still better, Pamphile—two in front and one behind, eh? Tell Paddy to come out where I can see him."

"He is a devil," said Tom, with an oath. "Pat, come around in front. He will not run away, I can see that."

"Run away, Tom?" said Jean, in mild surprise. "Why should I do that?"

"Damned if I know," said Tom.

"You never saw me do it, did you, Tom?"

"No, damn you! Not yet."

"Not yet, Tom? Why do you say that?"

"Oh, be silent, Tom," broke in Pamphile. "Why all this talk? Don't you see that he is mocking you. Jean Baptiste Giroux, listen to me. We have certain requests which we desire to make."

"Requests, Pamphile?"

"Yes, requests. Demands, if you like."

"Demands? That is interesting. I am curious to know what they are."

"You shall know soon enough. Begin, Tom."

"Jean Baptiste Giroux, damn you!" spluttered Tom Sullivan. "You know damn well what I want, and if you don't give it up, by God, I'll kill you, you cursed thief— kill you, I say."

"Give up what, Tom?"

"The mail contract, damn you!"

"And if not, Tom?"

"If not? You refuse? He refuses. Come on, boys! All together!"

But Pamphile laid his hand on Tom's shoulder.

"Wait, Tom. He has not yet refused. Give him a chance. Wait, I say. I also have a request to make of Monseigneur the Bishop."

Jean did not smile any more; but his lips were pressed close together, and a steely glitter was in his eye.

P

"What is it, then?"

"I ask, Monseigneur the Bishop that was to be; I demand, little priest, to be permitted to strike you four times across the face with this little whip; the same, you will notice, that was used the other day. It was with some difficulty that I obtained it, but here it is—the very same, I assure you."

"And if I refuse?"

"If you refuse, little priest, I propose, for myself alone, not knowing what the good Tom may wish: I propose to tie you to a tree, without clothes, of course, and to flog you within an inch of your life. For my part, I would not kill you, but I might leave you for the mosquitoes."

"That would be pleasant," said Jean, as though deliberating. "Unique, too, in this part of the world. I do not like it, at all. And you, Paddy, what would you do?"

"I?" said Pat, "I am sick of the whole damned business, but I stand with Tom. But I'll not see you killed, Jean, no, not that."

"I let you off easy last time, Paddy."

"So you did, Jean, damn well I know it. I'll not see you killed, Jean."

"Thank you for that, Paddy!"

With that Jean made a sudden spring across the path in front of Pamphile and Tom; made a feint at Pat's face with his left hand; and with his right dealt him a terrific blow at the corner of the jaw below the left ear. Pat fell to the ground, and lay unconscious among the ferns; while a struggle went on about him that he would have given his right arm to have seen.

Instantly Pamphile and Tom fastened upon Jean

like mastiffs upon a bear at bay. Both were strong men; but Jean shook them off, and tried to close with one alone. More wary now, they circled about him, out of reach of his powerful hands; but presently he regained the path, stood with his back to the rock, and they feared to come near.

"Come on, boys!" said he, with a grim smile. "I am waiting for you."

"Come on yourself, damn you!" yelled Tom Sullivan.

"All right, Tom; I am coming. You first, my friend," said Jean, as he advanced slowly upon Tom; keeping an eye and an arm for Pamphile, who was about to take him in the rear. This time Tom, who was one of the best fighters in the parish, stood his ground; exchanged a feint or two with Jean; and then, nimbly evading a blow that should have felled him to the earth, he suddenly whirled; his body sank; his feet rose in the air, one after the other; and he delivered a furious kick at his enemy's head, the terrible *savate*, with which he had been known to split open an adversary's skull, and which, in the lumber woods, had won him the title of "Terror of the Gatineau." The fight would have ended then and there, but that Jean, who had been expecting the attack, swerved a trifle to one side; seized the lower foot, as it rose; and allowed Tom to fall by his own momentum on head and shoulders with such force as to drive the breath from his body and to leave him stunned upon the ground. Thus, frequently, the *savate*, if not successfully delivered, brings destruction to him who launches the blow.

As Tom fell, Jean received a blow at the back of the head that sent him to his knees; as he sprang to his feet he took another that made him reel; but the third blow he parried; also the fourth; and then he began to counter with such effect as to put Pamphile wholly on the defensive; and forced him back, step by step, now on the path, now trampling among the ferns, down to the stream and up the slope on the other side, until they stood upon the very spot where Pamphile, in the presence of Gabrielle, had been struck in the face and wounded in the soul.

"Here is the place. Well, Pamphile, have you had enough?"

Pamphile made no reply, but glared in futile rage, while his right hand still clutched the whip with which he had planned to take revenge.

"Ah, the little whip!" said Jean. "And you would like to strike me in the face? Well, you shall do so."

"What?" exclaimed Pamphile, in astonishment.

"I struck you in the face," said Jean, in a calm, even voice, "instead of killing you; and if it would be a satisfaction to you to strike me in return you may do it. Now—begin!"

A peculiar expression, as of a rat driven into a corner, came into the face of Pamphile, as he slowly raised the whip.

At this moment a shrill cry rang out through the woods —a woman's voice.

"Oh! Oh! Jean! Take care! Behind you! Look! Look!"

The warning came too late; for Pamphile, dropping the whip, sprang at Jean's throat; while Tom, who had crept up like a cat, seized him from behind; and together they bore him to the ground.

There they twisted, writhed and lashed about for moments that were like hours; but soon were still, for Jean was upon his knees; and then he rose, slowly, steadily, until he stood erect, with Pamphile still hanging to his throat, and Tom's strong arms clasped about his body. They were resting, as it seemed, taking breath for the final struggle; but presently nerve and muscle were tense again; the strain was on; they swayed to and fro, trampling the ferns, staggering against the trees, and all the while moving down the slope toward the stony bed of the stream. Pamphile and Tom, seeing this, and realizing that Jean meant to fall on them there, made a tremendous effort; and once more dragged him down. Then Jean, putting forth all of his great strength, rolled over and over down the slope; while his enemies, like bulldogs, hung on, now above, now beneath, until they all lay together in the stream, among the boulders and pebbles that in ages past had broken from the mountains and had been worn smooth by the incessant action of falling water. Pamphile lay beneath the weight of two men; but still his fingers clutched the throat of Jean, and slowly tightened until he could hardly breathe.

"Pamphile," he whispered, "let go, or I will kill you."

The grip tightened. Jean was being strangled to death.

With a last effort he rose to his knees, seized the head of Pamphile that was pressed against his breast, forced it back until it touched one of the large, smooth pebbles; and then, with a sudden jerk, cracked it like a nut against the rock. The head lay there with staring eyes and open mouth; the body relaxed; but still the fingers held their grip; and it was with difficulty that Jean released his throat from the dying grasp.

The fight was over. Jean staggered to his feet, in great distress of body and mind, his face all covered with blood and bruises; and turned to Tom, who still clung to him, looking up with expression of mingled hate and fear.

"Tom!"

"By God, I'll kill you yet," muttered Tom, making a last and futile effort.

"No!" said Jean, putting his hand on Tom's head, and pressing back the elastic curls of bright red hair. "No, Tom, old man, let us have no more killing. Oh, why did we do it, Tom, my friend?"

The terror fled from Tom's soul; the hate and anger too; and as he looked up at Jean's battered, sorrowful face, he broke down and wept like a child.

"Oh, my God, my God!" he moaned. "Why did we do it? Pamphile dead; Pat dead; and I, I might as well be dead too. My God! My God!"

"Pat is not dead, Tom. I hear him, I think. Yes, there he comes. Thank God. Pat is all right, Tom, and you are all right too. Brace up, old man. But Pamphile? *Mon Dieu!* What have I done? Tom, I am going away. You will look after Pamphile—you and Pat. There will be some expense—I will pay it. And the mail contract——"

"Damn the mail contract!"

"But no, Tom; it is yours now. You will drive the mail to-morrow, will you not? The mail must go— Her Majesty's Mail."

"Yes, I will do it, Jean; but it will be yours when you come back."

"I am not coming back, Tom. Good-bye."

"Jean Baptiste," said Tom, grasping the extended hand, "you have been damn good to us that have been damn mean to you, and it's damn sorry I am for all our damned cussedness. Come back soon, and we'll be good neighbours and friends, by God, we will."

As Jean strode along toward his home he saw Blanchette by the path, weeping bitterly.

"Ah, Blanchette, it is you. And you saw it all."

"Not all, Jean. I was too much afraid, and I hid behind the rock. Oh, why did I not stop it? *Mon Dieu*, but it was terrible! You are a hero, Jean Baptiste."

"No, Blanchette, far from it. A brute, rather, a species of tiger. At one time I would gladly have killed them all, and drunk their blood. *Mon Dieu*, what an uprising from the depths! But now that has passed; and the man, the Christian, is sorry for the deeds of the brute. But you do not understand such things, Blanchette."

"No? You think not? Ah, if it were only so. But I, too, have my struggles, my conflicts. But oh, Jean, you are hurt! Ah, my poor Jean, he can hardly walk. Lie down here, on the cool moss, and I will fetch some water from the stream. Ah, *Mon Dieu! Mon Dieu!*"

"No, I am all right. A little dizziness—that was all. It is gone now, and I must go. No, Blanchette, it is not I who need you, but Pamphile down there. For me, I could not touch him. Ah, the poor fellow! A strong man and brave; yes, brave to the last. *Adieu*, Blanchette."

"*Adieu!*" said Blanchette, going away; and then she turned, suddenly, fiercely:

"Jean!"

"What is it, Blanchette?"

"Nothing," she said, as she turned away down the path. "There was something, but I have forgotten. *Adieu*, my friend. May God keep you."

CHAPTER XXII

THE WILDERNESS

"MISERY loves company," they say. How true and yet how false! The miserable seek society as they take to drink, that they may forget their sorrow; but those who are sore hurt, with a pain that cannot be forgotten, a grief that will not be put aside, creep away to die, or to be alone, until the cruel wound is healed. They seek the solitary places, where they may have the silent sympathy of the stars, the unuttered consolation of the desert, the healing virtue of the wilderness; where they may renew their strength at the fountain of life, or return the worn-out body to Mother Earth, and the tired spirit to Father God.

So Jean Baptiste, failure, good-for-nothing, who had come to the end of all his efforts, had seen the ruin of all his hopes; humiliated, discouraged, deserted by lover and friend, despised and rejected, with the brand of Cain upon his forehead; fled from the dwellings of men to the solitude of the forest, to be alone with his wounded spirit, to fight alone the grim battle with the dark angels of grief, regret, remorse, and despair.

Within a stone's-throw of his mother's door was the edge of the great Laurentian forest, stretching northward without a break to the settlements of the Saguenay and Lake St. John, and thence north and north-west to the barren wastes of Labrador and the rocky shores of

Hudson's Bay. In that vast region are lonely places where trappers and Indians seldom pass and lumbermen have blazed no trail. There moose and caribou roam undisturbed; there giant pines grow on virgin hillsides; there lie lakes on which no canoe has ever floated; and there bloom flowers that are never seen by mortal eye. It is a retreat where one may be alone; a sanctuary where no enemy may come; a wilderness where one may be lost; but where one may find paths of peace, rest by still waters, restoration for the soul, and a meeting-place with God.

As Jean Baptiste, hunter and trapper now, with a pack on his back and a rifle in his hand, plunged into the forest, and the trees received him with open arms, the people and things that he had known seemed to go into the background of consciousness like the unreal images of a dream. It was as though he had died, and was awaking in a place where there were no people, but only trees and underbrush, ferns and moss, wild grasses and flowers, soft black soil underfoot, and a canopy of leaves overhead, with openings here and there, through which he could see the blue sky and white, fleecy clouds. The air was fragrant with moist, earthy odours, and the scent of flowers and leaves. Not a sound was heard, save now and then the call of a bird, the chatter of a squirrel, or the crackle of a breaking twig. So sudden and complete was the change that Jean thought of himself as another person, seeking refuge in a new world, but ever pursued by the avenger, his former self, whom he was vainly trying to leave behind.

On he went through the cool woods; winding about among the trees, clambering over rocks and fallen timber, and all the while going up the mountain-side, until a precipice rose before him, a wall of granite where there was no foothold, but only crannies here and there, with a tuft of grass or a sprig of fern growing in a handful of soil. Jean did not see that it was an impassable barrier; but set himself to it with blind force; went up a little way; and then fell, torn and bleeding, to the ground. Presently he took a new path, skirted the rock until he found a place where trees and shrubs could grow; and here he climbed, though with great difficulty, to the very top. It was a good omen, this victory after defeat; and it was with no little satisfaction that he stood upon the rocky crown of the mountain looking down on the valley below.

How small everything looked from an elevation of a thousand feet! The dwellings and barns were like dolls' houses; the cattle like mice; the chickens and ducks like flies; and all went about without a sound, like puppets in a pantomine. Driving along the road at a snail's pace, and raising a little cloud of dust, were a tiny horse and cart with a mannikin in the seat holding invisible reins in one hand and an invisible whip in the other. It was Bonhomme Gagnon, going to market with his butter and cheese, his potatoes and turnips. What a foolish little midget, with his pompous air, his absurd swagger and his boastful talk! And the other neighbours were much the same—tiny insects buzzing about in the sunlight of a summer's day, soon to be drowned in the rain or nipped by the early frost. Was it for the good opinion of creatures such as these that one should plan and work? Glory, fame—what were they? To hear one's name pronounced by the lips of men; to see them stare and gape as one passed by; and after that silence, and the pall of night. It was not worth while. Nothing was worth while but to escape from the world, to bury oneself in the forest, to ascend some high place whence one could look down and see the pettiness of everything—and then to go away and forget.

It should be easy to forget. One had only to ascend another thousand feet, and all those objects would disappear from sight, or one could turn away, plunge into the forest, and they would be gone. Thus one could at will obliterate the past, annihilate the world. True, but that would only bring them back again; for to the inward vision they would be as large as ever, prominent, imposing, dominant. When the former life was out of sight it was by no means out of mind. When the eyes were closed, the absent ones, friends and enemies, would return and take their accustomed places. To banish them would be to commit a species of suicide, a mutilation of the soul, like cutting off a hand or plucking out an eye. No, he who would have the fulness of life must forget nothing; and he who would be brave must not only face the future with courage, but look with steadfast eye upon the past. Thus Jean Baptiste, as he stood on the mountain-top, in view of his old home, allowed his former self to overtake him, and together they went on their way.

Jean made his way over the crest of the mountain, and down the northern slope, into a densely wooded valley, pushing through the thick fringe of alders that bordered the stream, floundering in a maze of swamps and beaver ponds, stepping lightly over carpets of thick, yielding moss in the shade of cedars and tamaracks, climbing up again among the beeches and maples of the middle slopes, the pines and spruces of the higher ridges, until he stood on the summit of a second range that overtopped all the southern hills. Looking back he saw beneath him a sea of hills and valleys, with the edge of a clearing showing here and there; while far away and beyond were the flats of Beauport, the great river, and the spires and roofs of Quebec shining in the morning sun. The gleaming light seemed to beckon, to call him back to a life and work that should lead in the end to the city, the centre of civilisation, the lure and reward of all worthy effort; but the spirit of the woods was strong within him, and he turned his back upon the achievements of industry and commerce, and all the idols of the market-place, and set his face once more toward the wilderness.

For many hours Jean marched along through the woods, steadily going northward toward the height of land that divides the waters flowing into the St. Lawrence from those that go into Lake St. John and the Saguenay; until at sunset he stood upon a low ridge and saw at his feet, in a hollow between the hills, the lake toward which he had been moving all the day. He smiled in satisfaction at the feat which he had accomplished; for he had taken a course across five ranges of mountains, and kept his direction with such precision that he came out of the forest within a hundred yards of the cabin that was to be his home.

A few eager steps brought him to the place, and there it was, in a clump of pines: a little hut of logs well caulked with moss, with a good roof of hollowed logs, and an excellent chimney of rough stones, a most unusual luxury in a trapper's cabin. It was the lodge of Michel Gamache, where he and Jean had spent many happy days; but where other hunters seldom came, for it was far in the forest, and the way to it was rough and little known.

The door was on the latch; and Jean went in; laid down his gun and pack; but immediately came out and took the path toward the lake. For a moment he turned aside into a dense growth of firs, and presently appeared again with a birch canoe on his shoulders, which he carried down to the shelving beach and placed in the water. Then he crept aboard, knelt in the stern, and with a long stroke of the paddle sent the light craft far out on the lake.

There was not a ripple on the water but the wavelet in front of the canoe and the long wake that trailed behind. There was not a living creature in sight but a pair of loons that floated beyond a rocky islet; and not a sound but their shrill, quavering cry that echoed and re-echoed in the hills. The granite rocks along the shore were reflected perfectly in the water, in all their colours — grey, blue, pink — and with all their covering of lichen, moss, grass, ferns, and trees. Birches with their silvery trunks, pines with their long branches, tall, spire-like spruces were there, pointing upward on the land and downward in the water; while above and below the trees was the red glow of sunset, and glorious clouds floated in an azure sky.

Presently the canoe shot into a long, narrow bay, where the shores came close together; the shadows met; and a panorama of new beauties unrolled at every turn. Here a flock of wild ducks rose quacking from the water and flew over the trees; there a long-legged heron stood in a marshy place among the rushes; there a doe and a half-grown fawn gazed in mild surprise, then leaped away and vanished in the woods.

Suddenly the bay came to an end where a stream flowed over a steep cliff into a deep, clear pool; and here Jean stayed for a while, listening to the music of the waterfall, watching the trout that lurked under the stones, and wishing for a rod and line that he might try a cast to see what would rise out of the depths.

Night was coming on as Jean turned the prow of his canoe down the bay; soon it was quite dark; and only the glimmer of stars on the water and the dense blackness on either side showed the way. Silently the paddle rose and fell; and on went the canoe through the darkness; until at the last turn, where the bay joined the main body of the lake, a bright light appeared over the trees; and the moon rose, making a shining path across the water. With powerful strokes Jean shot the canoe along the bright way to the very end; and plunged again into the shadow near the shore. Presently the light craft touched the landing-place, where Jean stepped out, pulled the canoe out of the water, turned it bottom up on the shore, placed the paddle underneath, and went up to the cabin.

After having fasted all day, Jean was hungry as a bear, and was glad to find in his pack the food that his good mother had provided. By the light of a candle he ate his evening meal; and then, spreading his blankets on a bearskin in the corner, and with his knapsack as a pillow, he lay down to sleep.

"Ah!" he said to himself, as the tension of muscle and nerve was relaxed for the first time since the early morning. "How tired I am! I did not think that I could be so tired. How good it is to rest at the close of a long day! And such a day! *Mon Dieu*, but it was a day, a good day!"

"What, Jean Baptiste?" said his other self. "A good day, you call it, when you have fought like a beast and killed a fellow-man, a brother, one who might have been your friend! Do you know what you are saying? Wake up, Jean."

"Wake up? But no, I prefer to rest, to sleep—a long, long sleep. And it was a good day. I have lived. Yes, lived."

"But what of Pamphile?" said his good angel, in a far-away voice.

"Pamphile? Pamphile?" murmured Jean, as he went into the land of dreams. "That fellow with the pretty face? He got it, did he not? Got what he deserved. Regret it? No! A good fight! A good day!"

CHAPTER XXIII

THE CURE

ALREADY the healing power of the wilderness had begun its work, and as the days passed Jean gradually recovered the tone and balance of mind that had been so much disturbed. Without knowing it he had been under a strain for a long time, that tension of brain and nerve so characteristic of modern life, which the strongest and most ambitious must endure, when they forsake the old ways and go out into the unknown to make new paths wherein the feet of generations to come may safely tread. In the vanguard of progress they do the work of pioneers; in breaking new ground they are themselves broken; and the army of civilisation marches on over their graves.

But Jean Baptiste had left his place in the front rank, and gone to the rear, to the very remotest rear, where there were no people and neither sight nor sound of war, where the forest was his hospital and Nature his physician. What wonder that he grew to love the quiet retreat, and to wish that he might never hear the battle-call again?

By night he slept a dreamless sleep, undisturbed by the cry of the loon, the hoot of the owl, the wail of the lynx, or any call of birds or beasts that hunt by night. He was up with the dawn, and out in the open, refreshed and strong, with bright eyes and a joyous heart, breathing the fragrant morning air, rejoicing in the free movement of every limb, his whole being expanding in the growing light, and leaping up to meet the rising sun.

To Jean the wilderness was as the garden of the Lord. All the trees that he loved were there, all the wild flowers of the season, with ferns and mosses of many kinds; there were bubbling springs and clear streams, shallow ponds and deep lakes, dense thickets and open glades, narrow glens and broad valleys, low ridges and high mountains, whence he could look out upon a sea of forest-clad hills stretching away and beyond to meet the circle of the sky.

But it was the lake by the cabin that Jean loved most of all, and there he spent many hours of every day in his birch canoe; plying long strokes of the paddle; skimming along here and there; exploring creeks and bays or floating in the shade of a rocky point, at the mouth of a stream or by a sunken log, while he cast a fly upon the water to lure the wary trout. When the lake was calm he could see not only the rocks and trees of the shore, but his own thoughts and feelings reflected there; for it was a mirror to his soul. When a wind came up and ruffled the surface with little dancing waves, his thoughts seemed to dance and sparkle in their turn; and he would sing the song of the voyageur to the hum of the breeze and the lapping of the waves. When a white squall came, raising great waves capped with foam, the soul of Jean Baptiste was stirred to its depths and rose up to meet the foe; as with a strong grip on the tough paddle he held the canoe to the wind and rode out the storm; mounting on the crest of the waves, beating down into the trough, splashed and buffeted, rocked and tossed; but all the time pushing on toward the lee shore, where at last he lay in calm water, serenely watching the tempest as it passed.

Like the human heart, the lake was never twice the same. Even at dawn it varied with the breeze, the mist, the clouds, the rain, the light of the waning moon, the gleam of the morning star. All the days were different, each from the others; so also the nights. Now the lake was a crystal, now a pearl, now of a pale turquoise blue, now blue like a sapphire or green as an emerald; and often, at sunset, it was like an opal with fire in its heart, changing soon to violet and purple tints, and then taking on the deep indigo of the evening sky, shot with points and threads of gold. Even on sunless days, when the clouds hung low and rain fell, there was a pensive beauty in the lake, like the sweet, pale face of a nun trying to forget the light and love of bygone days in thinking of the glory that should appear in the eternal world. Truly, thought Jean, it was good to be in the wilderness, and gladly would he live and die beside a lake like this.

Jean was alone in the forest, and yet he had many companions. One who goes carelessly through the Laurentian woods sees few signs of life, and hears few sounds; though many eyes watch him, and many creatures come out of hiding when he has passed by. To Jean, trained in woodcraft from his early years, the timid creatures showed themselves and spoke in many tongues. Not only the bold blue jay and the camp-robber came about the cabin; but the red-headed woodpecker, the chickadee, the wren and the waxwing came; the crossbill, too, the linnet and the wood-thrush—all curious to see the strange being that lived there, and eager to pick up any crumbs that might be lying about. Chipmunks came every day; sometimes red squirrels; now and then a marten; and often, in the twilight, a porcupine came, shuffling along, rattling his quills, and nosing about for scraps of fish and bacon to add to his meagre diet of bark and roots.

Not far from the cabin was a pond where a colony of beavers played and worked every night, diving, swimming and splashing about, slapping the water with their tails, climbing about on the embankment, or venturing into the woods to eat pieces of juicy bark or to gnaw patiently at the trunks of young birches that were to be timber for building and a store of food for the long winter. There were mink and otter, too, in various places; and Jean would have made war on them as enemies of the trout, but that he wished to leave them for trapping later in the year, when the skins would be in prime condition and would fetch high prices in the fur market at Quebec.

All the wild animals came, at one time or another, to the lake. Almost every evening Jean saw red deer drinking there; occasionally a caribou; and once a moose, with great branching horns and outstretched muzzle, calling loudly to his mate, came to the end of the point, plunged into the water, and swam over to the other side. There were lynx and wild-cat in the forest that at times made a fearful noise by night. There were foxes, too; a few lone wolves; and now and then a vagabond bear, seeking for honey, nests of ants, raspberries and blueberries, catching a hare or a marmot now and then, and glad to make a meal of dead fish or carrion when he could find such dainties.

All these and many more, the hunter and the hunted, came and went; some with rush and clamour; others silently and on tiptoe; but always leaving some token of their presence by which Jean knew that they had been near. In the evening and morning twilight he caught glimpses of them as they passed; by night he knew them by the sounds they made, the odours they exhaled, or their bright eyes glowing in the dark; by day he saw their tracks in the soft earth, the marks of teeth and claws on the trees, the remains of their feasts, and all the signs of life and death that tell the joyous and fearful tragedy of the forest.

Jean had a mind to take part in the tragedy, to be one of the characters of the play; and the more he thought of it the more alluring it seemed. Not only could he lead an independent and enjoyable life in the woods; but he could obtain a good income from the sale of skins; and even accumulate a small fortune, if he had good luck. He had traversed the forest in every direction for a distance of twenty miles or more, and had carefully estimated the probable catch of a winter's work. There was scarcely a pond in all that region where there were not scores of muskrats; and although the price of a single skin was not high, they would be worth a good sum in the aggregate. Of more valuable fur-bearing animals there was that old stand-by, the beaver; with the skunk, the mink and the otter; squirrel and weasel; wild-cat and lynx; wolf and bear; red fox and hare—all of which were well worth taking for the skins alone, not to mention the meat, which was excellent food in the cold weather.

Then there was the marten, or Hudson Bay sable, a rare and valuable fur; and finally, and most highly prized of all, the black or silver fox, which often sold for fabulous sums; as much as a thousand dollars being paid, at times, for a single skin. In his explorations Jean had seen the marten several times; and knew of a place on a sandy hillside that was the home of a whole family of silver foxes; for one morning he had seen father, mother and four cubs playing, like kittens, on the carpet of pine-needles near their hole. Yes, he could make a good living in the wilderness, preying upon the beasts of prey.

Cruel? True; yet no man can say that without hypocrisy but the vegetarian; he who eats neither meat nor fish; wears neither wool, silk, leather, nor garments trimmed with fur. But if we must defend the trapper, let us say that for every fox that he takes a hundred hares are kept alive; and that by killing a single otter he saves the lives of a thousand trout. Moreover, while the beasts resemble man in some respects, they are by no means human. They suffer some pangs when they come to die, but during their lifetime they are not continually haunted by the thought of death. The king of terrors has no terror for them; and at the end they lay down their life without regret, and with no fear of torment in any life to come. It is as though the good God in pity had given them compensation for having withheld the gift of reason: the knowledge of good and evil which is at once the glory and the shame of man, the source of his profoundest joy and sorrow, his salvation and damnation. Which of them would not rather be one of the beasts that perish, than a man, made in the image of God, fated to follow evermore the gleam of an ideal that might lead to the heights of eternal glory, or the bottomless abyss of eternal degradation and loss?

As for Jean Baptiste he accepted cheerfully the law

of life and death as it was in the wilderness. He would live there, as the others did, according to his strength and cunning; and he would kill, too, not wantonly, but for a purpose; and when his strength failed, through sickness, accident or old age, he would lie down to die, as they did; with a few moans, perhaps, but without any vain regrets. What is death, after all, that men should fear it so? In the midst of the amenities of civilised life it seems a dreadful thing to die; but in the forest it is the merest incident. The good God cares for sparrows; gives them food and drink and everything else that they need; and after a while takes away their breath. So also He cares for man. The generations come and go; the earth abides; and God lives. Life and death, both are good; for living or dying we are the Lord's. Thus Jean Baptiste learned the lesson of the wilderness.

At the same time Jean was learning another lesson; for he was getting a distant view of himself and his past life; and seeing everything, as he thought, in the true perspective. He was lifted up, at times, into a kind of third heaven; where he had such a vision of eternal values, that the world of men, with all their thoughts and feelings, their words and deeds, seemed little and far away. The friends and neighbours seemed like puppets in a show, and his own part in the play as vain and futile as the rest. The work that he had done, the plans that he had made, the ends for which he had striven, no longer seemed desirable or worth while. He cared no longer for the opinion of men, whether good or bad; for any help that they might give him, or any harm that they might do. No longer did he hate his enemies or love his friends. The place where he had lived and the people he had known had lost all power over him; for the thought of them caused neither satisfaction nor regret, neither joy nor sorrow, neither hope nor fear. His own personality, even, had lost its value; for the memory of the past was fading away; the outlook was narrowing; and he was living in the present only; borne along upon the tide of time, his individuality lost in the great ocean of existence of which he was so small a part. He was intoxicated by the thin air of those altitudes, and deceived by the illusions of the mountain-top.

From this plane of thought Jean descended suddenly and with something of a shock to solid earth, on one of those cold, grey days of August that come to remind us that summer is passing, and that soon the snows of winter will begin to fall. Instinctively he went about the cabin and found many gaping chinks that should be filled with moss. He looked at the wood-pile, and saw that it was almost gone. He examined his store of provisions, and saw that it was running low. Firearms, fishing-tackle, traps, snowshoes, traineau, clothes, moccasins—all required attention, for the cold season was coming, and it was necessary to be prepared. Already the beavers were preparing for the winter, and the human animal knew that he must do the same; for the wilderness is kind to those who keep her commandments, but implacably cruel to those who will not live according to her law. So Jean determined to rest and play no more; laid philosophy aside; spent the day in the forest, chopping dry wood for fuel; and in the evening, by the light of a blazing fire, he sat down to mend the traps of Michel Gamache.

CHAPTER XXIV

THE RELAPSE

THE novitiate of Jean Baptiste was at an end; and now he was about to renounce all that he had held dear in his past life; and to take the final vows of the wilderness. It was as though the spirit of some remote ancestor had taken possession of him, body and soul, and was leading him back and down to the primitive savagery out of which the race, by long effort and much pain, had gradually ascended. He was a willing captive, feeling neither surprise nor regret; and it was with a sigh of relief that he cast the burden of civilisation away; and laid him down to sleep upon his bed of fragrant balsam; to dream of the green trees, clear streams, placid lakes and purple hills of that pleasant summer land.

But in his dreams the former self of Jean Baptiste awoke, and came unto his own. He had wandered far; and was almost lost in the wilderness; but suddenly he found himself walking along the familiar valley road, passing the old landmarks, and approaching the old home. The night was dark; but the house was lighted; and as he entered by the open door, he saw a company of neighbours and friends sitting in a circle around the spacious kitchen; the men smoking, and the women knitting, as they often used to do in the good old days. But now there was no telling of stories; and neither song nor jest nor laughter; but a subdued and orderly conversation, like a memorial service in honour of one who was dead. No one looked up as Jean entered, walked across the room and took the vacant chair; and there he sat as a ghost, seeing and hearing everything, but himself an unseen and unbidden guest.

His mother rose to pass the spruce-beer and cakes; and when she came to Jean's place she paused and smiled as though she saw him sitting there and smiling in return.

"Oh!" she said, "I think that Jean is not very far away. We shall see him soon, I am sure."

"Let us hope so," said Father Paradis, gently, "but I fear that he will never return. He is a disappointed man. He has missed his vocation, he who might have become a bishop, an archbishop, a cardinal, even, in the course of time. What a pity!"

"Yes," said Michel Gamache, "to miss the path like that, he who might have been a great man in the parish, a seigneur, a member of Parliament—anything. And now he is a failure, a *coureur des bois*, like me."

"And all for the sake of a girl!" broke in Blanchette. "As though there were only one girl in the parish, in the Province. What folly! No woman is worth it. He is a fool, that Jean Baptiste."

"He is more than that!" cried Pamphile, who sat by the fire, pale and haggard, his head bound up in a shawl. "He is a coward, that little priest. A coward, I say; and he fears the law. The law, yes, and this little whip across the face. *Sacré!* If he returns he shall suffer. I say it; I, his ancient enemy."

"And I," said Bonhomme Laroche, shaking his fist, "I wish to see him too, that proprietor, debtor, thief. He will not pay me? Well, I have the mortgage. See!

There it is, Madame, the mother of a thief. My mortgage! My property! My farm!"

"No, you old miser!" shouted Brother Nicholas. "You shall have your money, but no farm of ours. Do not cry, my mother. Do not think of the old miser, nor of Jean, the deserter. He was to have stayed at home; he, the youngest; but now I have returned. Fear nothing. I am with you, I, Nicholas."

"Yes," said Bonhomme Gagnon, rising in his place. "Yes, Madame Giroux, we will assume the responsibility—I, Telesphore Gagnon; you, Nicholas; you other children; you neighbours; everybody. As to Jean Baptiste, forget him, the good-for-nothing. He was too proud, he, and the good God could not endure it. It is the good God who has driven him away, and he is lost, lost."

At this Madame Giroux began to weep, while Father Paradis tried to comfort her, and Brother Nicholas was sending all the people home; when suddenly at the open door appeared a sturdy figure in a brown fishing suit, with a pannier on his back and a lance-wood rod in his hand. It was Monsieur Trudel, the City Man.

"What is this?" he exclaimed. "Is it a funeral, a wake, or what, in the name of God? My brave Jean, where is he? Dead? Gone away? A fugitive, he? Deserter, you say? Failure? Good-for-nothing? Thief? Murderer? Ha! Ha! It is to laugh! Reassure yourself, Madame. It is not in Jean Baptiste to be like that, he who conquered me, the champion of the Province. He will return, most certainly, and soon. *Mon Dieu!* He is here now. There, do you not see him? There, in the chair! Jean, my brave one! Arise! Show yourself!"

During all that time Jean had sat there speechless, immovable; but now, with a mighty effort, he rose in his place; stretched out his arms and cried, in a strong and joyous voice: "Monsieur, my friends, my mother, I am here!"

Jean advanced with outstretched hands toward his friends; but they shrunk back, pale and terrified, into the dark corners of the room and out of the door; until there was only one left, a slight figure in a brown fishing suit, with pannier, and rod, reddish-golden hair, violet-blue eyes, and a radiant smile.

"Monsieur Trudel," he began, "you have changed much since, since—— *Mon Dieu!* Gabrielle! It is you, you! Come to me, dear."

But the vision melted away, and Jean awoke to find himself standing alone on the cabin floor in the glimmering dawn of a new day.

"*Mon Dieu!*" he said to himself. "Was it a dream? I can see them still, when I close my eyes—and hear them, too. They think of me, talk of me, those good friends, whom I had forgotten—almost. They are disappointed in me, it would seem, and with reason. But they had expected too much—more than I could do. What? More than I could do? Oh, Jean Baptiste, it was not that you could not, but that you would not! What is that one cannot do? 'Good-for-nothing? Too proud? The good God does not like it?' How does Bonhomme Gagnon know that? I should like to show him, the old rascal, that the good God will aid me to resume my former work. By Heaven, I will resume!

"I am a dreamer, it would seem. Yes. A coward? No! Afraid of the law? I had not thought of it.

The law ? Why then ? For the killing of Pamphile. But I did it in self-defence. Tom and Paddy will witness. Will they ? *Dieu!* Possibly not. And what then ? A trial, a judge, a jury, and I, the accused at the bar. It might be well to remain here, or to go to the Indians of Mistassini or Hudson's Bay. Then I should be a *coureur des bois* indeed ; an exile, fugitive, outlaw. What then could I say to the abuse of Bonhomme Gagnon, Monsieur Laroche, and the rest ? Coward — thief — deserter — good-for-nothing — fool —all that and more ! Yes, I should deserve it all.

" 'And all for the sake of a girl ? ' Blanchette, that was unjust. It was a combination of circumstances, an accumulation of misfortunes, that drove me away—for a time. O, Blanchette ! I have many good excuses, as you must know ; yet I will excuse myself no more, for I think I hear you say : ' *Qui s'excuse s'accuse !* '

" But Gabrielle was there, and oh, what a lovely smile ! To see her again I would return, in spite of everything. But where was the garb of the Ursulines— the black robe, the hood, the veil, the rosary, the cross, the pale face of the novice, the nun that is to be ? There was none of that. No, it was only the City Man after all. Gabrielle was not there, for she was not thinking of me, but of Jesus and Mary and the glories of Heaven. But if she gave a thought to me, and a single call, I would enter the convent and take her away—from the altar, even—and who should hinder me ? An adventure that, worthy of a knight of the olden time. Yes, worthy of those times, perhaps ; but for a penniless habitant, a trapper, a discredited fugitive, not quite so suitable. To steal a novice from the convent, an heiress—a noble deed, surely. Ah, Gabrielle, why so much haste ?

Why bury the heart before the love is dead ? A little more time, a year, two years at most—that is all I ask. Could you not grant me this, Gabrielle ?"

As Jean thought of the situation from every point of view, the difficulty and perplexity of it seemed to increase, and no way of escape appeared. He walked up and down the narrow cabin like a wild beast in a cage, raging and wondering at his fate, wildly longing to break away and be free. At last, unable to disentangle the coil, he threw it from him, flung open the door, and went out into the open air.

It was like going into another world. The clouds of yesterday, the gloom of night, the ghostly dawn, all had passed away; and the summer morning, fresh and lovely, opened like a flower. It was good to breathe the pure, fragrant air; to see the earth, the grass and the trees in all their brightest colours, washed by the rain; to hear the sweet voices of the forest; and to feel, in every nerve and muscle, the strength and courage of returning day. In the lake Jean took his morning plunge, and a long swim far out in the deep water; and when, an hour later, he returned to the cabin, refreshed in body and soul, with a keen appetite and a joyous heart, he was ready to face the world, to receive its hardest buffets, and to deliver his most telling blows in return. The soldier was himself again; his furlough was over; and he was going back to the front.

Jean was now ready to do battle with the enemy, for he was at peace with himself. The long struggle within him was at an end; for his nobler self had obtained the victory, and taken complete control. The strange, weird voices that had well-nigh led him astray for ever were heard no more. The voice of fear, too, was stilled; for he was so completely possessed with the thought of his work and the joy of devotion to his cherished ideal, that there was neither fear nor doubt in his soul; but strong courage and sublime faith that the work of his hands would be established, and that the day of small things would have a great and satisfying fruition.

Jean's attitude toward the world was changed. No longer did he despise the opinions of the neighbours, but found himself wondering what they would think and say when they saw him take up his former work. His mother, the curé, his friend Michel, and a few others would be glad; and he was glad to think that he could please them in any way. His enemies would be disconcerted; and he took a malicious pleasure in thinking of their confusion, and in guessing what their next move would be. As for the rest, they might find fault for a time, but sooner or later the benefits of his work would appear; all the good people of the parish would approve; and his reputation would spread far and wide—to Beauport, Quebec and the greater world beyond. A good name—that was something worth while; a prize to be won, a possession to be kept, an heirloom to be handed down to future generations. But if not, if in the end he should fail, he would still have the satisfaction of attempting a noble task; a few friends would understand, and the good God would know that he had done his best.

And Gabrielle? Jean could no longer think of her as a novice of the Ursulines preparing to take the veil, to renounce all human love and devote her young life to prayer and penance within convent walls. On the contrary, she now resumed her former place in his scheme of life; the golden-haired chatelaine of his Castle in Spain; for whose love he would fight unto the death; at whose feet he would lay all the trophies of war; and from whom he would ask, in the hour of victory, his greatest earthly reward—herself.

As Jean was preparing to depart, putting away the canoe, setting the cabin in order, taking a last look at the lake, he was sorry to leave the beautiful place; but his heart was full of an abiding joy; for he was thinking all the time of Gabrielle; and when at last he turned his back upon his hermitage, and set himself to climb the southern hill, his joyous voice woke again the echoes of the forest, as he sang the brave song of a crusader who prayed for victory and love:

> "Partant pour la Syrie,
> Le jeune et beau Dunois,
> Alla prier Marie
> De benir ses exploits.
> 'Donne, reine immortelle,'
> Lui dit-il en partant,
> 'Que j'aime la plus belle,
> Et sois le plus vailiant.'"

CHAPTER XXV

TREASURE TROVE

"WHERE are you going, Jean Baptiste?"

Jean stopped instantly, and stared in dumb surprise; for there was Gabrielle standing before him in a hunting suit of tanned buckskin, a light rifle on her arm—a veritable Diana of the wilderness.

"Speak, Jean! Say something, for goodness' sake. I am not a ghost, nor a holy picture descended from its frame. It is I, Gabrielle."

"As I see," said Jean, raising his cap and offering his hand. "Welcome to Lac Desir, Gabrielle."

"Lac Desir! What a pretty name! Where is Lac Desir, Jean? Which way?"

"Come, Gabrielle; I will show you. It is only a step or two. I was coming away, but now I will gladly return. This way, if you please. It is a rough path, and steep. Take my hand, will you not? Now we are at the foot of the hill, and there, under the trees, is the cabin—my hermitage. It is not much like the Ursulines, I should say. You were there, were you not?"

"Yes, certainly, I was there for a while; but I have escaped, as you see. I could not say so many prayers— it was too fatiguing—and I had to have a little vacation in the country. Soon I will return."

"Return?" exclaimed Jean, in dismay. "That would be a pity. Do not return to the convent, Gabrielle."

R

"Why not, then? It is a pleasant place, the convent, so quiet, so peaceful; and the sisters are so good, so dear. And it is a place where one can make one's salvation."

"Salvation, you say, in a convent, in a little cell? How can one find that between four walls? It is something that belongs to the open air, Gabrielle; something that comes with the sunshine. No, it is here that one finds true peace, rest for the soul—salvation, if you like."

"But you are going away, Jean. Is it possible that you are leaving your salvation?"

"But no. I have found it here; and I am taking it back to St. Placide, to the work that awaits me there. But now that you are here I forget all that, and I could stay for ever. Stay here, Gabrielle."

"So I will, Jean, for a few moments, at least. It is a pretty place. But where is the lake? Where is Lac Desir?"

"We are coming to it. Another turn of the path and you will get a glimpse of it through the trees. There, there it is!"

Gabrielle clapped her hands.

"Beautiful! Charming! Like a picture—more lovely than any picture! Certainly, the pictures at the convent are not like this. You have a canoe, of course. Get it, Jean—quickly. You shall take me out on the lake."

"With pleasure, Gabrielle. The ship is here, in this clump of spruces. It would not be easy to find it if one did not know the place. I am revealing all our secrets, as you see. Presently I will give you the keys, and you shall be the sovereign lady of these dominions. Look! A fine canoe, is it not? Of a single piece of bark. It is not often that one sees a canoe like this—so light, so graceful, so strong, so perfect in all its lines. One carries it like a feather. There, I will place it in the water, by the rock. Have the goodness to take your place in the bow, Mademoiselle the Passenger. A great honour for the canoe, for me, I assure you, Mademoiselle."

"Monsieur, it is with sincere pleasure that I accord you the honour. But how complimentary you have become! Already you are recovering from the surprise, the shock, of my arrival. How serious you were a moment since! I thought I should have to cry. Smile a little, Jean. There, that is better. Once more. Now we are all right. How lovely the water! How balmy the air! How pleasant to glide along like this! Not so fast, Jean. Slowly. It is still early in the morning. Let us not think of time. Let us forget the world. Ah, now I know what it is to be dead to the world, as they say in the convent, and yet very much alive. I think that I have never lived before. But what would Mother Sainte Anne say if she could see me now? And why don't you ask how I happened to come?"

"It is enough to know that you are here, Gabrielle. If only you would stay."

"I am staying, am I not? But if you say that again I will go away at once."

"Allow me to remind you, Mademoiselle, that we are at some distance from the shore."

"But I can swim quite well, Monsieur; and if you provoke me I will jump into the water."

"As you did once before, many years ago. How well I remember the occasion! Do it again, Gabrielle, that I may have the pleasure of saving your life. Then you would belong to me, you know."

"What nonsense you talk, Jean! I will not jump into the water, just to please you, but I will go back to the shore all the same. Take me back."

"Oh, not yet, Gabrielle. It is too pleasant here. Never before have I seen the lake so beautiful. There was always something lacking; but now it is complete, perfect."

"It is truly wonderful, Jean; and it would be a pity not to enjoy it while we may. I like to sit here on this comfortable bearskin, dipping my hands in the water, looking at the trees, the sky, the clouds—while you do all the work."

"And I, Gabrielle, I should like to do this kind of work for the rest of my life, to glide along over a summer lake while looking into the face of one so beautiful, so——"

"Jean, I will splash you if you say any more."

"Do so, Gabrielle. I need a bath, perhaps."

"On the contrary, you look as though you took a bath every day, like a certain Englishman at Quebec. Is it possible that you have been here for a whole month? You are no wild man of the woods at all. I am disappointed in you, Jean."

"I am sorry, Gabrielle. In the future I will try to please you better."

Gabrielle blushed and looked away; while Jean, in tender and eloquent words, began to confess that he had loved her long; that in all his plans he had thought of her; that all his battles had been for her sake; and that it had been the hope of his life to lay his honours and trophies at her feet. When she went away the light of his life had gone out; and the world, once so full of beauty and interest, had become an empty, barren desolation. Now that she had returned, in all her radiant beauty, the glory had come back to earth; and the wilderness had become a paradise, a garden of love. How wonderful the forest! How enchanting the lake, nestling in the bosom of the hills! How blue the sky! How clear and pure the air! How glorious the freedom of the wilderness, far from the world, but near to the heart of Nature; near, also, to God. And if two loving hearts, by chance, by fate, by the will of God, found themselves together in such a paradise, was it not the will of God that they should make their home there; live upon the bounty so lavishly provided; conquer the wilderness; and achieve something unusual, unique, even, in their day and generation? A good living was assured; a fortune was not impossible; and the effort, the adventure itself, would be well worth while. Their ancestors had carved a kingdom in the forest — why not their children of a later generation?

Thus Jean Baptiste, like all lovers since the world began, saw everything through a golden mist that made a halo about his beloved; gilded the commonest objects with all the colours of the rainbow; and filled his eyes with a light that never was on sea or shore.

Gabrielle listened, as though fascinated, to the story of love; blushes came to her cheeks, smiles to her lips, and tears to her eyes at the wonder and beauty of it; her heart glowed in return; and she was on the point of stretching out her hands in glad surrender to one so strong, so brave, so noble, with such undying faith in her, in himself, in God.

Had Jean but known, he would have spoken of love alone, whom all hearts love, to whom all yield as to their dearest friend; but in his ignorance and folly he went on to speak of things external, foreign, out of harmony with the thought of love. Plans, ambitions, a good living, a fortune, the conquest of the wilderness—why all that? One must live, of course; but why speak of it at such a moment? The beauties of Nature—why so much of that? The lake was lovely, to be sure; the forest and the hills as well, on a summer morning such as this; but what would they be when winter came with its pall of snow and its chill winds blowing out of the North? And how forlorn it would be, far from the old home, with neither friend nor neighbour near; while the snow drifted high, an impassable barrier between the lonely cabin and the outer world.

Renounce the world? The dear, friendly world of St. Placide, the gay, joyous world of Quebec? As well might one enter the convent; for there, at least, one would have the society of the good sisters, the occupation of teaching, and the joy of devotion and worship when the congregation lift up their hearts and voices unto God. What could one do in the forest during the long winter with no books, no games, no music, no society? The ancestors were satisfied? True, but times had changed, and a new generation had arisen. Why go back to those half-savage days? Love? That was all very well now and then; but there were times when one did not wish to love, nor to be loved; when one might wish to cry, perhaps, and there would be no comforter, no one to console. Work? Yes, one might do that—cook, for example; or make garments of fur; or mend the traps; or chop wood for the fire.

Yes, that was what Jean wanted—a wife to do the work of a slave, to grow old with toil and hardship. Well, let him find an Indian squaw for that; and not ask a girl from a comfortable home to share his savage existence in the wilderness.

As Jean talked on, in his idealistic, unpractical way, about the glories of life in the forest, the crude realities of that life were borne in upon Gabrielle; and her heart was hardened against one who could, in the name of love, demand so great a sacrifice and offer so little in return. The smile faded from her lips, the colour from her cheeks, and the love-light from her eyes; while a grey cloud passed over the sun; and a chill breath from the North swept over the lake. Gabrielle shuddered.

" Take me back, Jean. I am cold."

" But, Gabrielle, it is so lovely here."

" I do not find it so. Take me back to the shore."

" But the sun will be shining again in a moment; and the lake, the forest, the hills, will be all aglow in the morning light."

" It will not. I detest your lake, your mountains, your forest. It is a desolation, and I hate it all—all."

Without a word Jean turned the prow of the canoe toward the shore; and when they reached the landing-place Gabrielle stepped out unassisted, and walked swiftly up the path, past the cabin, and on up the hill down which she had come an hour before. Jean noted the way she was going; and a few moments later he took up his pack and rifle, and with long, swift strides followed her trail up the ridge, and down the long slope on the other side. Presently he caught a glimpse of her through the trees, as she tripped along, lithe and active as a deer; and it was with no little difficulty that he kept her in sight until she came to the foot of the slope, and began to climb the shoulder of another hill. There Gabrielle slackened her pace, and turned on her pursuer with flushed face and angry eyes.

"Jean, Monsieur Giroux, I will trouble you to cease following me."

"I am sorry, Gabrielle, but I cannot let you go this way alone. It is dangerous at times."

"I am not at all afraid, and I wish to be alone."

"But you might lose your way, Gabrielle."

"I will not. I know the way quite well."

"But it is easy to get lost, Gabrielle, in this vast forest; among these hills, these cliffs, these marshes; and there are places where one might fall, and not be able to rise alone. One needs a companion."

"I do not. Will you please leave me?"

"I will not leave you, Gabrielle, until you are with your friends."

"Why, why? *Mon Dieu*, why not?"

"Because I love you, Gabrielle."

Gabrielle paused for a moment, on tiptoe, like a frightened deer; and then sprang away, and went on with incredible swiftness up the hill; then along a level place for a while; then down another slope; winding about in a maze of trees and rocks, hills and valleys; but all the time keeping, as she thought, the same general direction toward the place where her friends had set their camp.

An hour later Gabrielle found herself standing on the crest of a hill looking down upon a lake that shimmered in the sunshine, with tiny waves that sparkled like a cluster of diamonds set in emeralds. It was Lac des Isles, no doubt, where they had camped the night before. But where was the camp? And where were the islands? There was but one island to be seen; and no camp at all—only a cabin half hidden in the trees below. Yet the place was strangely familiar. What? Where could it be? Was it possible?

Gabrielle turned in dismay, and there was Jean standing beside her.

"Monsieur Giroux, Jean, what is this? Where am I?"

"This is Lac Desir, Gabrielle, and you are with one who loves you, dear."

Gabrielle looked up with a wistful smile.

"Are you sure, Jean, that you love me as much as you love the lake, for example; or the forest?"

"Oh, Gabrielle, it is you that I love, and you only."

"Or the life of the wilderness, Jean; and the struggle, the conflict, the conquest?"

"Gabrielle!"

"Or the pretty log cabin down there, Jean; or that lovely canoe all made of one piece of bark, so strong, so graceful, so perfect in all its lines. Or——"

"Hush, dear," said Jean, taking her in his strong arms, and kissing her on the wayward lips again and again, while her flaming cheeks and loving eyes, her quick breathing and the fluttering of her heart, told better than any words that she loved this man and would go with him to the end of the world.

By-and-by they went down the hill together; and as Jean was showing Gabrielle his home in the wilderness, she looked up in his face with an expression of perfect trust and whispered her confession of love and unconditional surrender.

"Jean, we shall be happy here. You will be my world and I yours. Two worlds should be enough for us; quite sufficient, should they not?"

"But no, dear. That was a foolish plan, a species of insanity, I think, a madness that came upon me. We will spend the honeymoon here, if you consent; and after that we will make our home in St. Placide. It will be a modest home at the first, but it will be the beginning of great things. There is only one obstacle, one danger; but we will not think of that. Nothing shall come between us any more, Gabrielle."

"Obstacle, Jean? Danger? I cannot think of any. But wait. Do you know why I came here? I had quite forgotten. Can you guess?"

"Gabrielle, I had not thought of it. Strange, too, that you should find your way to Lac Desir, so far from home. But you were nearly lost in the end."

"No, not lost, Jean, for you found me; and I, I found myself. Not lost at all, Jean Baptiste Giroux. But how did I arrive in the first place? Guess!"

"How can I? You did not know the way. No one knows it but Michel and I. Now I see. It was Michel who showed you the way, came with you. Where is he, then?"

"Good guess, Jean. You are not so stupid, after all. Michel and my father are down there at Lac des Isles, not five miles away. That explains my early visit, as you see."

"Perfectly. It is the best way to come. You take the old road to Lac des Isles, and then you follow the valley right up to this place. An easy way, Gabrielle, and yet you missed it. It is to laugh."

"No, indeed, I did not miss it on the way up, and if I missed it on the way back it was your fault, Jean. It was cruel of you to torment me like that."

"True, Gabrielle, and I am glad of it. If I had let you go alone you would have been lost."

"Not at all, Monsieur Giroux. I should have gone back to the happy Ursulines, to Mother Sainte Anne, and all the dear sisters, who would have received me with open arms. And I should not have said a single prayer for you, not one."

"No matter, Gabrielle. Now that I have you I shall have the benefit of your prayers as well; shall I not, dear?"

"No. Yes. I don't know. You will need them, without doubt; for you are a great sinner, Jean."

"How so, Gabrielle?"

"You broke the heart of that good girl, Blanchette."

"No, Gabrielle; not intentionally, at least. Moreover, I think that the heart of that young lady is not so very fragile."

"What do you know about it, stupid man? It was broken indeed, but now it is mended again—completely."

"Mended?"

"Yes, and she is to marry Pamphile Lareau."

"Pamphile is dead, Gabrielle."

"No, Jean. He is alive and almost well. For a time it was thought that he would die, but Blanchette brought him back to life, with the aid of the good God. That is what I came to tell you. We thought that you would like to know."

"Thank God!" said Jean. "And thank you, too,

Gabrielle. Now there is not a cloud in the sky. What a day, this—the best day of my life! And you came to tell me the good news."

"Yes, and to have a little outing, a little fresh air and exercise—after the convent, you know."

"Gabrielle, I am glad that you did not stay in the convent. It is a refuge, a blessed retreat, for those who are discouraged, for the weary, the sad at heart; but for the young, the strong, the brave, the world is a better place. It was not for you. You had no vocation."

"That is just what Mother Sainte Anne said. She is a dear friend. 'Listen, Gabrielle,' she said, 'for the voice, the true call that speaks to the heart. You shall know it by the tone, like the clear, pure sound of a bell, to which all the chords of the heart respond; and you will say: "Lo! that is for me." Sometimes the call of love is the voice of God, my dear.' Yes, she is a true friend, Mother Sainte Anne."

"And Michel. He also is a good friend to us, as to my father in the early days."

"Oh, Jean, there is something else that I was forgetting. I forget everything now. A treasure, a great treasure."

"I could not touch it, Gabrielle."

"No, Jean, you could not. But what do you think Michel has done? He has given it to Mother Sainte Anne to found a hospital for poor children, a cause that she has had at heart for many years. The poor children will be happy with Mother Sainte Anne, and she with them. I am so glad that you did not take the gold, Jean. Now it is treasure in Heaven. I call it Mother Sainte Anne's dowry and my ransom."

"Your ransom, Gabrielle? Yes, that is it. How lucky for me that I did not take the treasure!"

"And for me, Jean. Oh, how fortunate! I thank God! It was a miracle, almost."

"Yes, Gabrielle, but there is a greater miracle, the miracle of your love, and a treasure more precious—yourself."

"A treasure, I? Oh no, Jean, only a wilful, wayward girl. Can it be that you love me, Jean? Is it true?"

"Gabrielle!"

"Jean!"

THE TEMPLE PRESS LETCHWORTH ENGLAND

www.ingramcontent.com/pod-product-compliance
Lightning Source LLC
Chambersburg PA
CBHW020400080526
44584CB00014B/1108